MEDIA AND VOTERS

MEDIA AND VOTERS

The Audience, Content, and Influence of
Press and Television at the 1987
General Election

WILLIAM L. MILLER

CLARENDON PRESS · OXFORD
1991

Oxford University Press, Walton Street, Oxford OX2 6DP

Oxford New York Toronto
Delhi Bombay Calcutta Madras Karachi
Petaling Jaya Singapore Hong Kong Tokyo
Nairobi Dar es Salaam Cape Town
Melbourne Auckland
and associated companies in
Berlin Ibadan

Oxford is a trade mark of Oxford University Press

Published in the United States
by Oxford University Press, New York

British Library Cataloguing in Publication Data
data available

Library of Congress Cataloging in Publication Data
Miller, William Lockley, 1943–
Media and voters: the audience, cont t, and influence of press
and television at the 1987 general election / William L. Miller.
p. cm.
Includes bibliographical references and index.
1. Elections—Great Britain. 2. Great Britain. Parliament—
Elections,—1987. 3. Mass media—Political aspects—Great Britain.
I. Title.
JN956.M54 1991 324.941'0858—dc20 91–12899
ISBN 0–19–827377–0

Typeset by Hope Services (Abingdon) Ltd.
Printed and bound in
Great Britain by Biddles Ltd,
Guildford & King's Lynn

PREFACE

THIS book uses data from the 1987 British Election Campaign Study (BECS) for an in-depth analysis of the role of the media in contemporary British politics. I would like to thank the Economic and Social Research Council (ESRC), the Independent Broadcasting Authority (IBA), and the University of Glasgow for providing roughly equal funding for this study. I also owe a debt of gratitude to many friends, colleagues, and students who helped make the BECS study possible. Detailed comments on proposed questionnaires were received from Hugh Berrington, Keith Britto, Ivor Crewe, Glyn Mathias, Geraint Parry, Jorgen Rassmussen, Mallory Wober, and others. David Broughton acted as Research Assistant for the survey and Niels Sonntag for the associated content analysis of television news. Duncan McLean acted as Operations Manager for the panel survey. Linda Martin acted as Project Assistant. Questionnaires and manuscripts were typed and retyped at lightning speed by Elspeth Shaw and Avril Johnstone. Interviewing was done by a team of over 200 students from Glasgow University who worked far harder and more effectively than we had any right to expect. Roger Jowell, Sharon Witherspoon, Tony Heath, and John Curtice generously gave access to respondents originally interviewed for the 1986 British Social Attitudes Survey or the 1983 British Election Survey.

A description of the BECS study has been published as W. L. Miller, H. D. Clarke, M. Harrop, L. Leduc, and P. F. Whiteley, *How Voters Change: The 1987 British Election Campaign in Perspective* (Oxford: Clarendon Press, 1990) which provides a general overview of the study and a general introduction to political change during, and immediately prior to, an election campaign. The present volume concentrates exclusively on a more extended analysis of the role of the mass media in the electoral process. Special thanks are due to Mallory Wober and Martin Harrop, both of whom read the present manuscript and made numerous helpful suggestions, many of which I have incorporated into the text. Michael Lessnoff read the final chapter with a critical but helpful eye. I am most grateful for all their suggestions but the errors of fact and interpretation that remain are my own. *Media and Voters* is intended to be a self-sufficient analysis of the media during the 1987 election campaign and the months preceding it, but readers will find our more wide-ranging study, *How Voters Change*, a useful introduction to this more specialist work.

W.L.M.

Glasgow,
September 1990

CONTENTS

ABBREVIATIONS USED IN THE TABLES

Alln	Alliance
BES	British Election Study
BSAS	British Social Attitudes Survey
Con	Conservative
DK	Don't know
EXC	Excitement (motivation for following the campaign)
5.45	ITV's early evening *News at 5.45*
FF	First Fortnight Wave of interviews
GEN	Generalized. Generalized interest in politics was measured in the Mid-Term Wave. Generalized measures of regular media use were measured in the Pre-Campaign Wave. The wordings of these questions made them non-time-specific, however.
GUID	Guidance (motivation for following the campaign)
Highbrow paper	*Telegraph, The Times, Financial Times, Independent, Guardian*
I	For information about issues
INF	Information (motivation for following the campaign)
L	For information about leaders
Lab	Labour
Left-wing paper	*Mirror, Guardian*
Lib	Liberal
Lowbrow paper	*Sun, Star*
MID	Mid-Term Wave of interviews
Middlebrow paper	*Mirror, Today, Express, Mail*
NA	not asked
Nat	Nationalist
Nine	BBC's main evening *Nine O'Clock News*
NU	Not used
PEB	Party Election Broadcast

x ABBREVIATIONS

POST	Post-Election Wave of interviews
PRE	Pre-Campaign Wave of interviews
REINF	Reinforcement (motivation for following the campaign)
Right-wing paper	*Express, Mail, Star, Sun, Telegraph, The Times*
RS	BBC's *Reporting Scotland* (early evening regional news)
RSQ	Squared multiple correlation which equals the percentage of the variation in the dependent variable that is explained by the set of predictors shown in the table
SF	Second Fortnight Wave of interviews
Six	BBC's early evening *Six O'Clock News*
ST	ITV's *Scotland Today* (early evening regional news)
Ten	ITV's main evening *News at Ten*
V	For vote-guidance

Predictors Used in Multiple Regression Tables

Age	Measured on a three-point scale: old (over 55), middle-aged, and young (under 35)
Alln ident	Alliance identifier (= 'supporters' plus 'leaners'; see Appendix)
BBC–TV	BBC–TV news (or watched BBC–TV news)
Discussion	Frequency of political discussion
Con ident	Conservative identifier(= 'supporters' plus 'leaners'; see Appendix)
Education	Measured by the level of highest qualification attained, on a six-point scale, ranging from none up to a university degree
Excitement	Excitement-seeking motivation for following the campaign
Guidance	Vote-guidance-seeking motivation for following the campaign
Highbrow paper	Consistent reader of highbrow paper throughout the period 1986–7
Information	Information-seeking motivation for following the campaign
Interest	Political interest

ITV	Independent Television News (or watched Independent Television News)
Lab ident	Labour identifier (= 'supporters' plus 'leaners'; see Appendix)
Num TV	The number of different TV news programmes respondents said they watched 'regularly', ranging from 0 up to 12
Partisanship	In correlation and regression tables this is always an abbreviation for 'strength of partisanship', never for 'direction of partisanship'. See also the Appendix on use of the term in this book
On left	Respondents describing themselves as being on the left
On right	Respondents describing themselves as being on the right
Preference	Degree of preference, defined on p. 21
Radio 4	BBC Radio 4 News (or listened to BBC Radio 4 News)
Reinforcement	Reinforcement-seeking motivation for following the campaign
Right/left	A spectrum, with centrists treated as intermediate between right-wingers and left-wingers
Rt paper	Read right-wing paper
Strength ident	Strength of party identification

All correlations in tables are Pearson correlations multiplied by 100 to eliminate decimal points.

Entries in multiple regression tables are standardized multiple regression coefficients sometimes called 'path coefficients'. They have been multiplied by 100 to turn them into percentages and eliminate decimal points.

FIGURES

FIGURES xiii

TABLES

1
Models of Media Influence

Theories about the mass media's influence in politics have gone through three mutations which can be described as the *propaganda model*, the *minimal effects model*, and the *consumer model*. (For overviews of research on media influence in Britain see Negrine, 1989; Harrop, 1987; or, more briefly, Newton, 1990. For a transatlantic comparison see Dye and Zeigler, 1983. For a more theoretical discussion see McQuail, 1987.)

The *propaganda model* was popular between the wars (Jowett and O'Donnell, 1986, ch. 5; O'Shaughnessy, 1990, ch. 2). Media analysts looked back to the development of propaganda warfare by the British (soon followed by others) in the First World War. They were impressed by contemporary exponents of modern propaganda techniques in fascist Italy and Germany. Great claims were made for the effectiveness of this propaganda. Its content, from atrocity stories spread by the British during the war to Nazi films of the Nuremberg rallies in the 1930s, was self-evidently dramatic. On the other hand, survey research was still in its infancy and there was little firm evidence of any kind about the dynamics of public opinion. In the absence of evidence, speculation was unrestrained. Writers who assumed that they and their readers could take a dispassionate view of propaganda none the less felt sure that the mass public could easily be duped by it (Lippmann, 1922; Lasswell, 1927).

In 1940 Paul Lazarsfeld and his collaborators set out to reveal the power of radio propaganda in a more democratic setting— a presidential election campaign (Lazarsfeld, Berelson, and Gaudet, 1944, further developed in the 1948 edition; and Katz and Lazarsfeld, 1955). Lazarsfeld's team were pioneers of modern survey research methods. But instead of confirming the propaganda model as they had expected, their research led to the establishment of a new orthodoxy: the *minimal effects model* (Berelson, 1959; Klapper, 1960). They found that remarkably few citizens changed their voting intention during the long American presidential campaign, and even those who did change tended to cite the influence of friends, neighbours, and conversation partners rather than the mass media. Attitudes did tend to crystallize during the campaign as the previously undecided began to make up their minds, but they did so in ways that correlated more with their social position than their exposure to the mass media. Old social alignments were reactivated as the campaign reached its climax. So, within a presidential election context at least, mass propaganda seemed to have little effect.

That restriction is significant. Democratic elections permit, even encourage, the articulation of alternative viewpoints. Lazarsfeld and his colleagues stressed the importance of selective exposure to the mass media. Faced with a multiplicity of sources, citizens are not entirely passive recipients of media messages. They choose what to read and what not read; they choose whether to listen to a radio programme or not. Indeed, there seems much truth in the old proverb that 'there are none so deaf as those that will not hear'. Even when the radio is turned on, listeners can filter out and suppress unwelcome messages while paying particular attention to those they like.

This idea of selective exposure was later developed into the 'uses and gratifications' or *consumer model* of media influence (McQuail, 1987, p. 234; Blumler and McQuail, 1968; McLeod and Becker, 1974). This third model treats the reader, listener, or, more recently, viewer as a more active participant in the communication process. It is not enough to ask *whether* citizens have been exposed to a particular political message: it is necessary to ask *why* they have been exposed to it and *what* they hoped to get out of that experience.

Indeed, the whole question of media influence should be studied in the broader context of citizens' relationship to politics. Some are extreme partisans. Their view of politics is dominated by a powerful sense of identification with a particular party and they feel a strong sense of loyalty towards it. For them, the main purpose of reading the papers and watching television may be to find arguments to support their own party's case, to *seek reinforcement* rather than guidance. Others have weak or non-existent party ties. For them the concept of reinforcement is meaningless since they have no party loyalty to reinforce. They may read the papers and watch television news primarily in order to help decide how to cast their vote—that is, they may consciously *seek guidance*.

Yet others may be simply uninterested in politics, with neither a strong sense of party loyalty nor any great motivation to judge the claims of rival parties. They may buy a newspaper to read the 'small ads', the sports section, or the arts and entertainment pages. They may watch—if that is not too strong a word—television news simply because the TV set is on and they cannot be bothered to turn it off. Such citizens may be relatively insensitive to the media's political content, but relatively unresistant to its political message when they detect one. They may *seek information* or even *entertainment* rather than guidance or reinforcement.

No doubt there are other categories within the mass media audience. The essential idea of the consumer model is simply that there is a variety of motivations for media exposure and that motivations condition the message. The same article or programme can affect different people in different ways. Readers and viewers can use the media for their own purposes.

Studies of political participation have shown that psychological involvement with politics, if not actual participation, is generally associated with relatively high levels of 'socio-economic resources'—primarily income and education. Actual participation is influenced by this personal psychological involvement but also by more institutional mobilizing factors that encourage even the relatively uninvolved citizen to participate at least in easy forms of political activity such as voting or following political news in the mass media (Verba, Nie, and Kim, 1978).

The electorate's social and political background is likely to influence their interest in politics, their motivations for using the media, and the extent and type of their media exposure. The highly educated are more likely to read the highbrow press, to be interested in politics, and to be knowledgeable about political affairs. The highly partisan are more likely to use the media for reinforcement than for guidance. Similarly, social and political background factors are likely to affect perceptions of politics and the extent to which media content is able to alter these perceptions. Strong partisans, using the media for reinforcement, are less likely to be swayed by its content.

Of course, the arithmetic has to add up. We may discover larger media effects among some categories of voter than among others, but that does not increase the total of voters influenced by the media. Lazarsfeld's finding that few switched between presidential candidates in the 1940 election cannot be challenged by the consumer model. If some categories in 1940 were more flexible, more open to media influence than average, then it follows that other categories must have been even less flexible than average. So in a very stable electorate the consumer model may be valid but insignificant because the iron law of averages dictates that large changes can only occur in very small subgroups.

Yet the contemporary British electorate is not stable. Long-term studies of party loyalty suggest that the strength of British partisanship fell by half between the 1960s and the 1980s. The class basis for voting choice has also weakened: the strength of alignment between Labour and the manual working-class versus the Conservatives and the non-manual middle class has also halved over the same period. Arguments about the changing nature of social classes—the increasing professionalization of the middle class and fractionalization of the working class—only serve to underline the decay of class politics in Britain. The split among the Labour Party leadership in the early 1980s, the formation of the Social Democrats, and their subsequent Alliance with the Liberals widened the range of credible alternatives open to the British electorate and further weakened old loyalties. The result of all this has been a highly volatile electorate. Our five-wave panel survey of changing opinion in the 1980s found that half the British electorate indicated a preference for two or more of the three main parties at different times in that decade (Miller et al., 1990, ch. 1). At least half the contemporary electorate therefore merit the title 'floating voters'. So the potential scope for media and other short-term influences is large. The contemporary British electorate is much less stable than the electorate depicted in Lazarsfeld's study of 1940s America. It is characterized by change rather than stability. (See McLeod, 1988; McLeod and Blumler, 1987, on the changing social context of media influence.)

We can bring together these initial expectations about the role of the media by setting out a general model of the causes and consequences of media use. The model places voters' use of the media within a broader context of their approach to politics. It treats the media as both a dependent and an independent variable. People 'use' the media for their own purposes but are

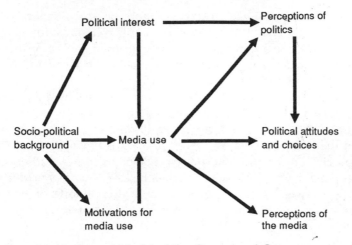

FIG. 1.1. A General Model of the Causes and Consequences of
Media Use

none the less influenced by it. The model can by represented
diagrammatically as in Figure 1 or stated as follows:

Socio-political backgrounds influence voters'
    1. interest in politics, and
    2. motivations for media use.
Actual media use is influenced by
    1. socio-political background,
    2. interest in politics, and
    3. motivations for media use.
People's perceptions of the media, their perceptions of politics,
and their attitudes towards politics are influenced by
    1. their media use, but also by
    2. their interest in politics, and
    3. their socio-political background.

Inevitably there is a degree of circularity in this model. this
decade's political attitudes form part of the next decade's political
background. (McLeod, Pan, and Sun (1990) propose a broadly
similar model and apply it to a sample of Wisconsin voters.)

The rest of the book investigates how this model applied to the
British electorate during the 1987 election campaign. Chapter 2
looks at interest in politics and motivations for following the
campaign. It looks at patterns of political involvement and how

those patterns changed under the mobilizing influence of an approaching election. What kind of people were most interested in politics? Were different types of people interested in politics at different times? Who sought reinforcement, guidance, information, or excitement in the campaign?

Chapter 3 looks at how citizens used the mass media. It asks who read what papers and who watched different television channels. More than that, however, it looks at continuities and combinations of media use. How stable was newspaper readership? How compartmented were television news audiences? Does it make sense to describe someone as a 'Guardian reader' or a 'BBC viewer'? Or do people change their habits or use so many media simultaneously that such categorizations prove misleading?

Opinion surveys in the 1950s rated newspapers as the most important source of political information but since the 1960s they have consistently identified television as the most important (Harrop, 1987, p. 53; IBA, 1987, p. 17). Chapters 4 and 5 focus on the content of television news during the election campaign. Chapter 4 looks at national television news taken as a whole. Chapter 5 distinguishes between BBC and ITV as channels, between early evening news and the main evening news, and between national news and regional news. Is there any objective evidence of bias on television news? Was the BBC biased compared to ITV? How did regional news compare with national news?

Chapters 6, 7, and 8 look at the impact of the media. Media style and content influence public reactions towards the media itself. Chapter 6 shows that viewers and readers clearly develop views about the medium as well as the message. They assess the usefulness of different elements of the media for their own political purposes. They judge them informative or uninformative, biased or unbiased, useful or useless. While these assessments owe something to personal needs and even to blind prejudice, they also owe something to the media itself. Did people find the media biased? Did they find it useful for providing information or guidance? Which elements of the media scored best for usefulness? Which electors found the media most useful?

Chapter 7 looks at the relationship between media content and changing public perceptions of the parties and the issues. Chapter

8 looks at the impact of the media on political attitudes and voting choice. What was the effect of newspaper bias on persistent readers? What was the effect of changes in the political agenda as defined by the press or, more especially, by television?

Finally, Chapter 9 relates our empirical findings to long-term but still active debates about the role of the media in a democracy.

The book is based upon a (stratified, clustered random) survey of the British mainland electorate (that is, excluding only Northern Ireland) coupled with a media content analysis. The survey was a five-wave panel study of the British electorate spanning the period from the early summer of 1986 until the week after the election in June 1987. Each member of the panel was interviewed up to five times, so we can track individual changes of attitude and behaviour as well as aggregate trends. The content analysis covered television news broadcasts during the second, third, and fourth waves of the survey.

The panel began with a round of interviews for the 1986 British Social Attitudes Survey, conducted mainly in April and May 1986. (See Jowell, Witherspoon, and Brook, 1987, for a full description of the sampling procedures and a full questionnaire.) We shall call this the Mid-Term Wave, because it occurred in the mid-term of the parliamentary election cycle. In 1987 we reinterviewed part of this sample during the week from Monday, 30 March, to Friday, 3 April. We shall call this the Pre-Campaign Wave of interviews. During the same week we video-recorded the *Six O'Clock News*, the *Nine O'Clock News*, and *Reporting Scotland* (the Scottish regional news) on BBC-TV, and *News at 5.45*, *News at Ten*, and *Scotland Today* on ITV.

On Monday, 11 May 1987, it was officially announced that there would be a general election on Thursday, 11 June. We recommended interviewing on Thursday, 14 May, and interviewed on each weekday (that is, excluding Saturdays and Sundays) up to and including the eve of poll, Wednesday, 10 June. There were therefore twenty days of interviewing between the announcement of an election and polling day itself. We shall call these day 1 to day 20.

During this short period of the official campaign we attempted to interview each respondent twice, once during the First Fortnight (days 1 to 10) and a second time during the Second Fortnight (days 11 to 20). We shall refer to the 'First Fortnight'

and 'Second Fortnight' Waves of campaign interviews as well as
to the subsamples associated with particular days. We paid very
close attention to the sequencing of interviews within each wave
in order to make each day's set of respondents an approximately
random subsample of the wave as a whole. Television news was
recorded from Tuesday, 12 May, (that is, two days before interviewing commenced) to Wednesday, 10 June—excluding Saturdays and Sundays as with the interviewing.

Finally, after the results of the election became known on
Friday, 12 June, we allowed our survey respondents to digest the
implications over the weekend before reinterviewing them for
the final Post-Election Wave, starting on Monday, 15 June. We
completed 92 per cent of the post-election interviews by the end
of that week and all of them by the following Wednesday.

All the 1987 interviews were done by telephone. However,
most of the respondents had been interviewed face to face in
previous surveys—either the 1983 British Election Study (BES)
survey or the 1986 British Social Attitudes Survey (BSAS). For our
Pre-Campaign Wave we reinterviewed 1,120 respondents from
the 1986 BSAS. We attempted to reinterview all of these respondents in subsequent waves. However, during the First Fortnight
Wave we added 447 respondents from the 1983 BES sample and a
further top-up of 350 new respondents designed to compensate
for BSAS respondents whom we had been unable to contact or
who had refused to be reinterviewed. This somewhat complex
panel structure is set out in Table 1.1.

The panel can be viewed and analysed in a variety of ways.
First, we can treat each wave as a whole. This gives a sequence of

TABLE 1.1. *Panel Structure* (no. of respondents interviewed)

	July–Aug 1983	April–May 1986	March 1987	Late May 1987	Early June 1987	Mid-June 1987
Short name for wave	NU	MID	PRE	FF	SF	POST
BES sample	3,955	—	—	447	389	386
BSAS sample	—	3,100	1,120	1,008	866	882
BSAS top-ups	—	—	—	350	263	277
TOTAL	3,955	3,100	1,120	1,804	1,518	1,545

cross-sections and allows an aggregate trend analysis based upon large samples. Second, we can subdivide each wave into the individual days within that wave (more often we use pairs of adjacent days or calendar weeks to get larger subsample sizes). This permits an aggregate trend analysis which is unfortunately based upon subsamples, but much more time-specific samples; so it allows a more detailed examination of fast-moving trends at the cost of increased sampling error.

Third, we can take data from two or more of the waves to construct a two-wave or multi-wave panel and look at how individuals (not just aggregates) changed their perceptions and attitudes. Once again there is a cost in sample size, since any analysis must be limited to respondents who gave interviews in *all* of the waves under study. However, this way of looking at the data does allow us to examine cross-currents of opinion and volatility which cancel out in the aggregate to reveal little or no net trend. This approach also has very great advantages for causal analysis.

Most analyses in this book are based upon the BSAS part of the sample in order to allow us to combine background variables from the 1986 BSAS interviews with media use and opinion variables from later waves. At different points in the book, however, we shall find it useful to adopt all three of these analytic perspectives—wave by wave trends, trends within waves, and multi-wave panels.

2
Psychological Involvement in the Campaign

By 'psychological involvement' with politics we mean feelings of concern, interest, and closeness which link citizens to political events, personalities, or institutions. Cross-national studies of political participation reveal a general tendency for psychological involvement with politics to be influenced by citizens' personal resources—primarily their income and education (Verba, Nie, and Kim, 1978; Barnes and Kaase, 1979). These socio-economic resources give them the skills and the opportunities to become involved.

At the same time these studies also highlight the significance of mobilizing factors—institutional rather than personal influences that encourage political involvement. Institutional factors very obviously affect actual participation: parties, for example, canvass citizens in their homes and encourage even the relatively uninvolved to go out and vote. But more than that, institutional factors also affect psychological involvement itself. Parties encourage a sense of party commitment, party loyalty, partisanship or party identification (the terms are interchangeable here). Partisanship is at once both personal and institutional in its origins. An important aspect of psychological involvement in its own right, it also affects other aspects such as interest and discussion as well as actual political behaviour such as voting.

Our concern here is not with generalities, however. Patterns may exist in general without operating in contemporary Britain. They can be weak or strong. They can vary in strength from place to place and from time to time. So these general findings provide only a basis for analysis in any concrete situation. Indeed, the general pattern is now so well known and understood that attention needs to be focused on variations rather than generalities. How far does the general pattern apply to the contemporary British electorate? Does its influence vary through time?

INTEREST AND DISCUSSION

Using our panel we can track the levels of political interest and political discussion through the months leading up to the election. In our Pre-Campaign (March 1987), First Fortnight (May 1987), and Second Fortnight (June 1987) Waves we asked: 'How interesting do you find what's happening in politics at the moment?' Respondents were offered a four-point scale for replies: 'very, fairly, not very, or not at all interesting'. At the same time we asked: 'How often, during the last week, have you discussed politics?' Possible replies were 'often, occasionally, very little, or not at all'.

A year earlier, in the early summer of 1986, the British Social Attitudes Survey (our Mid-Term Wave) also asked about political interest, but it framed the question in more general terms: 'How much interest do you generally have in what is going on in politics?' It offered a five-point scale for answers: 'a great deal, quite a lot, some, not very much, or none at all'. The change in question wording means that there is an inevitable discontinuity in the trend between 1986 and 1987.

Despite the problems of question wording, however, it seems clear that interest in politics peaked during our Pre-Campaign Wave and declined thereafter, while political discussion rose continuously from the Pre-Campaign Wave to peak at the end of the campaign (Table 2.1).

TABLE 2.1. *Trends in Levels of Political Interest and Discussion* (%)

	1986	PRE	FF	SF
Very or fairly interested*	60	72	58	62
Often or occasionally discuss politics	NA	51	69	73

* In 1986: 'a great deal' plus 'quite a lot' plus 'some'.

Although in general it might seem paradoxical that interest should decline as an election approaches we have to remember that even in Western democracies elections are not the only events that stimulate public interest in politics. During our Pre-Campaign Wave the Prime Minister, Mrs Thatcher, went on a very highly publicized and successful visit to President Gorbachev in Moscow while her Labour opponent, Neil Kinnock, went on a disastrous trip to see President Reagan in Washington. The splendid, quasi-royal atmosphere of Thatcher's reception in the Kremlin seems to have stimulated interest rather than discussion while the domestic party battle over familiar issues and personalities during the election campaign did the opposite.

Although the levels of interest and discussion clearly varied with the flow of political events we may ask whether the same people remained at all times the most involved or whether different people were more involved at different times. There was certainly a strong correlation between interest in politics in one wave of the panel and in the next, averaging 49 per cent. Similarly the correlation between frequency of political discussion in one wave and the next averaged 48 per cent. The correlation between interest and discussion within the same wave was rather less: it averaged 38 per cent. None the less, there was a considerable degree of coherence (interested people discussed politics) and consistency through time (the politically involved tended to stay politically involved) (Table 2.2).

TABLE 2.2. *Correlations through Time between Interest and Discussion*

	Interest in politics				Political discussion		
	MID	PRE	FF	SF	PRE	FF	SF
Interest							
MID	100	49	23	20	41	33	30
PRE		100	45	32	42	33	31
FF			100	51	20	34	25
SF				100	15	26	37
Discussion							
PRE					100	44	41
FF						100	52
SF							100

None the less these correlations, relatively strong though they are for social survey variables, are a long way short of 100 per cent and do not preclude the possibility that patterns of interest and discussion varied through time. Moreover, there is an intriguing puzzle in the table: mid-term interest correlated better with campaign-time discussion than with campaign-time interest. Indeed, as the election approached, the correlation between current interest and mid-term interest sank to a remarkably low level. By itself that suggests a considerable difference between 'being generally interested in politics' and 'finding the election campaign interesting'.

Two of the best predictors of political involvement within the panel were education and partisanship—in keeping with general expectations. But their correlations with political involvement varied significantly over time (Table 2.3) We measured education by the level of highest qualification attained, using a six-point scale ranging from none up to a university degree. Partisanship, or party identification as it is often called, was measured by whether respondents claimed to be party 'supporters' and by how strong a supporter they claimed to be, using a three-point scale of party support: very strong supporters, fairly strong supporters, and a composite of those who said they were either 'not very strong' supporters or not supporters at all. Strength of partisanship varied over time; for these correlations between partisanship and other aspects of involvement, we have taken partisan strength during the Pre-Campaign Wave.

TABLE 2.3. *Correlations between Political Involvement, Education, and Strength of Partisanship*

	Correlations with interest in politics				Correlations with political discussion		
	MID	PRE	FF	SF	PRE	FF	SF
Education	33	13	5	11	14	10	18
Partisanship	25	23	25	15	20	17	16

In the parliamentary mid-term there was a particularly strong correlation between education and interest but it declined very sharply as the election approached. The correlation between interest and partisanship was lower in the mid-term, but did not sink so rapidly. These trends hint at a switch from more personal

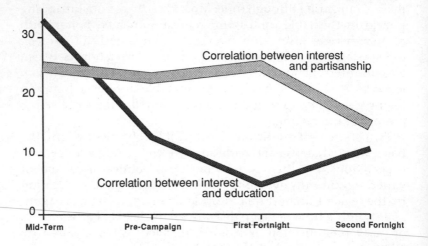

FIG. 2.1. Correlations between Political Interest, Partisanship, and Education (see Table 2.3)

to more institutional influences upon interest as the election approached.

One problem with these bivariate correlations between political interest and particular background variables is that background factors correlate with each other. Older people tend to be less educated but more strongly partisan, for example. Education also correlates with reading highbrow newspapers and with social class, both of which may have an independent influence on interest in politics. We can use multiple regression to reveal the independent effects of each background influence upon political interest once the others have been taken into account.

A preliminary regression analysis using measures of education, occupational class, class self-image, neighbourhood class, industrial sector, region, age, sex, religion, ideology, party choice, and newspaper readership to predict political involvement showed that many of these potential influences had little or no effect once the influence of other variables was taken into account. In particular, class was not a significant influence on political interest once education was taken into account. A much simplified

multiple regression will suffice, using only ideology and newspaper readership in addition to education and partisanship.

Ideology was measured (in the Pre-Campaign Wave) by whether
respondents said they were on the left, on the right, or in the
centre. Newspaper readership was measured on a three-point
scale placing those who consistently read a highbrow paper
throughout the period 1986–7 into the top category, those who
consistently read a lowbrow paper in the bottom category, and
everyone else in the middle. For this analysis, highbrow papers
were defined as *The Times, Telegraph, Financial Times,* and *Guardian.*
Lowbrow papers were defined as the *Sun* and the *Star.* Age was
measured on a three-point scale: old (over 55), middle-aged, and
young (under 35).

Multiple regression confirms the influence of education on
political interest in the mid-term and also the collapse of its
influence as the election approached. It also confirms the con-
tinuing influence of partisanship. Both left- and right-wingers
were usually more interested in politics than those who placed
themselves in the centre. Older people and readers of highbrow
papers were more interested in politics during the mid-term but
not significantly so at election time (Table 2.4).

TABLE 2.4. *Multiple Regression Analyses of Political Interest and Discussion*

Predictor	Political interest				Political discussion		
	MID	PRE	FF	SF	PRE	FF	SF
Education	31	12	0	7	13	9	15
Partisanship	21	17	23	16	16	13	14
Age	10	11	−5	−5	10	6	1
Highbrow paper	13	17	10	4	12	9	8
On left	26	15	20	16	14	15	17
On right	15	21	15	1	12	13	12
RSQ	25	15	10	7	10	7	8

These findings can be illustrated in more detail by looking at
trends in political interest. In the Mid-Term and Pre-Campaign
Waves political interest varied fairly steadily across the education
spectrum and it was markedly lower in the working class than in

ddle class. But by the end of the campaign political interest
ghtly *higher* in the working class and there was no significant variation in interest across the educational spectrum, except
for a slightly higher rate of interest amongst graduates. Those
with a degree were the most interested but those with only CSE
qualifications were next.

Similarly, in the Mid-Term and Pre-Campaign Waves readers
of the *The Times*, the *Telegraph*, and the *Guardian* were extremely
interested in politics while readers of the *Sun* and *Star* were
extremely uninterested; but by the end of the campaign there
was no significant difference between them—though more because highbrow readers lost interest than because lowbrow
readers' interest went up (Table 2.5).

TABLE 2.5. *Trends in Political Interest by Education, Class, and Newspaper
Readership*

	% 'very interested' in politics			
	MID*	PRE	FF	SF
Educational qualification				
Degree	52	36	23	29
Other professional	27	30	18	17
School A levels	31	28	9	17
School O levels	21	26	15	11
School CSE	12	24	13	21
None	14	22	15	17
Class				
Middle class (non-manual)	26	30	17	17
Working class (manual)	16	20	14	19
Paper read consistently (1986–7)				
Guardian	54	43	15	16
Telegraph/Times	34	48	20	15
Express/Mail	20	28	12	18
Mirror	20	27	17	19
Sun/Star	12	11	7	14
None	18	23	11	16

* Figures for the Mid-Term Wave comprise those saying 'a great deal'
plus half those saying 'quite a lot'.

At all times 'very strong' party supporters had above average levels of political interest and 'fairly strong' supporters usually had intermediate levels of interest, though those who denied being party supporters at all were usually a bit more interested than the weakest party supporters. People who placed themselves at the centre of the ideological spectrum had very low levels of interest but it made little difference whether they placed themselves out on a wing or merely claimed to lean towards that wing. (It made a lot of difference in terms of party choice but not in terms of political interest; see Table 2.6.)

TABLE 2.6. *Trends in Political Interest by Partisanship and Ideology*

% 'very interested' in politics

	MID*	PRE	FF	SF
Party support				
Very strong	35	46	32	34
Fairly strong	15	27	14	17
Not very strong	16	15	3	7
None	16	19	12	11
Ideology				
Left	29	26	19	26
Centre left	32	30	18	22
Centre	12	17	8	13
Centre right	22	30	18	16
Right	21	29	15	15

* Figures for the Mid-Term Wave comprise those saying 'a great deal' plus half those saying 'quite a lot'.

Political discussion increased sharply between our Pre-Campaign Wave and the campaign itself. Within the final campaign period from mid-May to mid-June discussion continued to increase. In the Pre-Campaign Wave, 19 per cent said they had discussed politics 'often' in the last few days. By the first two days of the campaign in mid-May this had risen to 30 per cent and in the last two days before the election it reached 42 per cent.

Socio-political background variables by themselves never predicted levels of discussion as well as they predicted levels of interest. However, we might expect them to influence discussion through interest. Education or partisanship encourages an interest in political affairs and that interest, in turn, encourages discussion. At the same time, education may have a direct effect upon discussion, independent of any influence on interest, simply because education provides the skills and information necessary for a discussion of current events. We can test this by using multiple regressions to predict levels of discussion based on the same range of predictors we used to predict political interest, but now using political interest itself as an additional predictor. These regressions show that the prime determinant of political discussion was political interest. But, over and above that, education, partisanship, and a clear ideological position (whether left or right) had some influence. Age and newspaper readership did not (Table 2.7).

TABLE 2.7. *Multiple Regression Analyses of Political Discussion*

Predictors	Political discussion			Political discussion		
	PRE	FF	SF	PRE	FF	SF
Education	13	9	15	9	9	13
Partisanship	16	13	14	10	6	9
Age	10	6	1	6	8	2
Highbrow paper	12	9	8	6	6	6
On left	14	15	17	9	9	12
On right	12	13	12	5	8	12
Interest	NU	NU	NU	35	30	32
RSQ	10	7	8	21	15	18

Note: Interest is measured in the same wave as the level of discussion predicted.

MOTIVATIONS FOR FOLLOWING THE CAMPAIGN

During the last fortnight of the campaign we asked respondents about their motivations for following the campaign on television and in the press. Blumler and his associates have argued the need to see the audience as active participants in the news transmission process, who view television or read papers for their own purposes (Blumler and McQuail, 1968; McQuail, 1987; McLeod and Becker, 1974). This so-called 'uses and gratifications' approach to media analysis stresses the importance of audience motivations. We realized that electors might have multiple motivations, so we did not ask them to choose between alternative motivations but simply to say whether each of four possible motivations was a 'very important' reason for their following the campaign:

1. to remind you of your party's strong points (the *reinforcement-seeking* motivation);
2. to help make up your mind how to vote (the *vote-guidance-seeking* motivation);
3. to see what each party would do if it got into power (the *information-seeking* motivation), and
4. to enjoy the excitement of the campaign (the *excitement-seeking* motivation).

The most frequently cited motivation was information: 76 per cent said information was a very important motivation for them, 58 per cent said reinforcement, 47 per cent said vote-guidance; and only 21 per cent said excitement. Within the last fortnight of the campaign there was no obvious trend except that the percentage quoting excitement rose slightly in the last few days of the campaign.

Motivations were not mutually exclusive. In particular, there was a moderately strong correlation of 33 per cent between information-seeking and vote-guidance motivations, and 28 per cent between information-seeking and reinforcement motivations. This seems reasonable: information is required as a basis for either decision or reinforcement. Excitement seeking was different: it correlated only weakly with the other motivations (Table 2.8).

TABLE 2.8. *Correlations between Media-Use Motivations*

	Reinforcement	Guidance	Information	Excitement
Reinforcement	100	22	28	13
Guidance		100	33	15
Information			100	13
Excitement				100

Socio-political background by itself had only a small effect upon motivations. As might be expected, strong partisans were more likely to be motivated by excitement. Less obviously, education and partisanship had opposing effects on motivations though, as we have seen, they had quite similar effects on political interest. The highly educated were particularly *un*likely to seek reinforcement from the media while strong partisans were particularly likely to do so.

Political interest intensified each one of the four motivations. Those with high levels of interest in politics were more likely to seek reinforcement, more likely to seek media help in making voting decisions, more likely to seek information, and also more likely to follow the media coverage to enjoy the excitement of the campaign. Although education correlated positively with political interest, education and interest had opposing effects upon motivations, which were particularly striking in the case of reinforcement. The well educated were *less* likely to seek reinforcement in the media, but the politically interested were *more* likely to do so (Table 2.9).

TABLE 2.9. *Multiple Regression Analyses of Motivations for Following the Campaign in the Media*

Predictors	Motivation				Motivation			
	REINF	GUID	INF	EXC	REINF	GUID	INF	EXC
Education	−14	−8	2	−3	−16	−9	0	−5
Partisanship	11	−4	0	20	7	−7	−5	16
Age	0	−4	−5	3	2	−3	−3	−2
Highbrow paper	−4	−7	−3	1	−5	−8	−5	0
On left	7	0	3	7	3	−4	−2	2
On right	4	2	7	−4	4	2	6	−4
Interest	NU	NU	NU	NU	24	22	30	28
RSQ	4	2	1	5	10	6	9	12

Undecided people were the ones with the most objective need for vote-guidance. In our Pre-Campaign, First Fortnight and Second Fortnight Waves, we asked our panel to give us 'marks out of ten' for 'how inclined' they were to vote Conservative, Labour, Alliance, and, if they lived in Scotland or Wales, Nationalist. The difference between the top two marks they awarded the parties is a measure of their *degree of preference* for their first choice over their second. Those who gave their first choice a much higher 'mark out of ten' than their second should have had little need of 'vote-guidance' from the media or anywhere else since their minds were already made up.

Degree of preference correlated most strongly with vote-guidance seeking, and rather less strongly with information seeking and excitement seeking; it was almost totally uncorrelated with reinforcement seeking. As expected the correlation with vote-guidance seeking was negative as, indeed, was the correlation with information seeking: that is, the greater their preference for their first choice over their second, the *less* likely citizens were to seek either information or, especially, vote-guidance. By contrast the correlation with excitement seeking was positive: that is, the greater their preference for their first choice over their second, the *more* likely citizens were to follow the campaign for excitement (Table 2.10).

TABLE 2.10. *Correlations between Degree of Preference and Motivations for Following the Campaign*

	Pre-Campaign Wave	First Fortnight Wave	Second Fortnight Wave
Vote-guidance	−13	−15	−20
Information	−10	−8	−11
Excitement	4	10	11
Reinforcement	−1	5	2

Note: Degree of preference = marks out of ten for inclination to vote for first-preference party *minus* marks out of ten for inclination to vote for second-preference party.

Multiple regression analyses show that degree of preference had a large, independent influence upon vote-guidance seeking but less on information and excitement seeking, and none on reinforcement seeking. We might have expected that degree of preference would do no more than substitute for strength of partisanship but that is clearly not so. Vote-guidance seeking seemed much more closely tied to voting preference than to

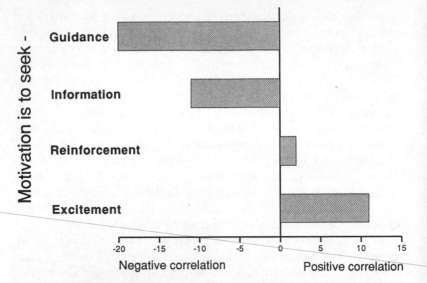

FIG. 2.2. Correlations between Degree of Voting Preference and
Motivations for Following the Campaign (see Table 2.10)

strength of partisanship, while excitement seeking seemed to be
influenced both by strong partisanship and by a clear voting
preference (Table 2.11).

CONCLUSIONS

Education and partisanship proved to be key variables for explaining political interest and all three were key variables in
explanations of political discussion or motivations for following
the campaign in the media. Degree of voting preference also
proved significant, especially in explanations of vote-guidance
seeking.

The influence of education on political interest declined sharply
as the election approached but the influence of partisanship did
not. Election-time interest was clearly very different from a more
general and persistent interest in politics. It was much more
dependent upon the mobilizing influences of party campaigning
and media coverage, much less dependent upon people's more
personal socio-economic backgrounds.

TABLE 2.11. *Further Multiple Regression Analyses of Motivations for Following the Campaign in the Media*

Predictors	Reinforcement	Guidance	Information	Excitement
Education	−17	−9	*	*
Partisanship	8	*	*	12
Highbrow paper	*	−10	*	*
Interest	24	19	27	29
Preference	*	−19	−9	10
RSQ	9	9	9	12

Note: In these regressions we considered the full set of predictors used for Table 2.9, but with the addition of degree of preference. However, by using stepwise regression we selected only those predictors that had a significant impact on motivations. Asterisks indicate predictors that had a significant impact on at least one motivation. Party preference, political interest, and media motivations were all measured in the Second Fortnight Wave.

Political interest had the most powerful impact on both political discussion and motivations for following the campaign, though education and partisanship were also influential. Partisanship encouraged discussion, and reinforcement seeking; it also made people more likely to enjoy the excitement of the campaign. Education also encouraged discussion, but it *dis*couraged reinforcement seeking and, marginally, discouraged following the campaign for excitement. A clear voting preference discouraged vote-guidance seeking, but encouraged excitement-seeking.

3

How People Used the Media

The British public has a wide choice of alternative news sources which includes national and regional daily papers, Sunday papers and weekly magazines, and radio and television programmes (Table 3.1). In 1986–7 nearly everyone tuned into BBC or IBA (ITV and Commercial Radio) news broadcasts but both organizations offered a wide range of alternative news and current affairs programmes likely to appeal to different audiences. The BBC, for example, offered short news inserts on its popular music channels Radio 1 and Radio 2 and in-depth extended news coverage on Radio 4. In 1986–7 it also offered in-depth reporting of regional news on channels such as Radio Scotland (though Radio Scotland news has experimented with a more 'popular' format since then). Each weekday, BBC television offered middlebrow newscasts

TABLE 3.1. *National Daily Newspapers in Britain, 1987*

Paper	Type	Readership (millions)	Preferred election result
Sun	Low	11.3	Conservative
Star	Low	4.0	Conservative
Mirror	Middle	9.0	Labour
Mail	Middle	4.5	Conservative
Express	Middle	4.4	Conservative
Today	Middle	1.0	Coalition
Telegraph	High	2.8	Conservative
Guardian	High	1.5	Labour
The Times	High	1.2	Conservative
Independent	High	0.8	No endorsement
Financial Times	High	0.7	Conservative

Note: Readership and preferred result taken from Harrop (1988). For circulation figures and preferred results at each election since 1945 see Harrop (1986), p. 139, or Butler (1989), pp. 94–5.

aimed at a large and heterogeneous audience—the early evening
Six O'Clock News and the main evening *Nine O'Clock News,* plus
lightweight coverage on its morning *Breakfast News* and in-
depth coverage on its late-night *Newsnight,* and middlebrow
regional news on programmes like *Reporting Scotland.* So the
broadcasting equivalents of particular papers were something
much more specific than simply the BBC, perhaps more specific
even than a BBC channel. We shall therefore find it useful to focus
on individual programmes as well as on broad channels.

REGULAR AND CAMPAIGN AUDIENCES

In our Pre-Campaign Wave we asked our panel about their
'regular' use of media sources: did they 'read any daily morning
newspaper at least three times a week?', did they 'normally read
a Sunday paper?', did they tune in to particular radio and
television news programmes 'at least three times a week?' We
asked explicitly about television *news* viewing, rather than about
general television viewing, because previous research has shown
that attention is very content-specific. Enthusiastic news viewers
are not the same people as enthusiastic soap-opera viewers.
Indeed, those who watch television the most (in total) may be
relatively inattentive to news programmes and relatively un-
influenced by them. (See for example Chaffee and Schleuder,
1986; Gunter, Svennevig, and Wober, 1986, ch. 9; Piepe, Charlton,
and Morey, 1988.)

During the final campaign in May and June we asked more
specifically whether they had read a paper 'today', and whether
they had watched television news 'today' or 'yesterday'. Naturally,
our figures for reading and viewing audiences on any particular
day were a lot lower than our figures for 'regular' readers and
viewers since 'regularly' could be as little as one day in every
two. Moreover, a feeling that it was 'worthy' to take an intelligent
interest in the news may have inflated the figures for 'regular'
reading and viewing.

Only a quarter of the electorate said they did not read a daily
paper regularly but about 44 per cent had not read a daily paper
on the day when we interviewed them during the campaign.
Perhaps others read their morning papers in the late evening,
after our interviews, which were all conducted between 6 p.m.

TABLE 3.2. *The Pattern of Newspaper Readership* (%)

	Regular daily	Regular Sunday	Daily 'today'	
			FF	SF
Lowbrow	17	21	10	11
Mediumbrow	35	27	28	28
Highbrow	15	16	12	13
Regional	4	9	4	3
None	25	25	44	43

Notes: A few respondents read combinations of papers or papers that were difficult to classify.

The *News of the World* and the *People* were defined as lowbrow Sundays, the *Sunday Times, Sunday Telegraph,* and *Observer* as highbrow. Regional papers include the Scottish papers except for the *Daily Record,* which is grouped with its sister paper, the *Daily Mirror,* as a middle-brow paper.

and 10 p.m. We did not detect any decline in overall paper readership during the final campaign itself (Table 3.2).

The audience for television news was high. Almost two-thirds of the electorate claimed that they regularly watched the BBC's main evening *Nine O'Clock News* and much the same regularly watched ITV's main evening *News at Ten* (Table 3.3). On any one day during the campaign the audience for BBC television news was slightly lower than that and the audience for ITV news substantially lower (Table 3.4). Traditionally, the BBC has been regarded as the proper channel to watch on state occasions—state funerals, royal weddings, and parliamentary elections. During the campaign, both networks broadcast extended news bulletins, so the audience's appetite for news may have been blunted before ITV's flagship bulletin, *News at Ten*, went on the air. British viewers regularly complain about the quantity, though not the quality, of election coverage on television (Gunter, Svennevig, and Wober, 1984; Gunter, Svennevig, and Wober, 1986, p. 70; BBC, 1987). And, of course, our definition of 'regular' viewing, 'three times a week', does not mean 'every day'. However, there is BBC–ITV audience research evidence that the audience

TABLE 3.3. *'Regular' Radio and Television Audiences before the Campaign*
(%)

	BBC	ITV
Breakfast TV news	21	23
Lunchtime TV news	26	18
Early evening TV news	63	46
Main evening TV news	65	62
Highbrow TV news (BBC *Newsnight/Channel 4 News*)	21	12
Regional TV news	46	38
News on Radios 1 and 2	39	
News on Radio 4	18	
News on Radios Scotland and Wales	4	
News on Commercial Radio		30

Note: Radios Scotland and Wales had a large audience for their news in their respective areas, but the Scots and Welsh electorates comprised only one-seventh of the British electorate.

TABLE 3.4. *'Daily' Television Audiences during the Campaign* (%)

	Watched today	Watched yesterday	Watched either today or yesterday
BBC-TV news	(36)	57	66
ITV news	(26)	40	48
BBC-TV or ITV	(49)	67	76

Notes: Figures based on the average audiences in our First Fortnight and Second Fortnight Waves. There was very little difference between the two waves.

Since interviews took place between 6 p.m. and 10 p.m. in the evening, many occurred before or during the mass-audience newscasts. Hence the much higher and more reliable figures for 'yesterday' than 'today'. Figures for 'today' have therefore been placed in brackets.

The BBC's own BARB/AGB figures suggest that on any one day in the first quarter of 1987, 69 per cent of the population watched some BBC-TV and 78 per cent watched either BBC-TV or ITV or both. These figures include some viewers who did not watch news programmes, however (BBC, 1988).

for both BBC and ITV news fell slightly between the pre-campaign period and the campaign itself (Reported in Blumler, Gurevitch, and Nossiter, 1989). Audience figures for different television news programmes during an election campaign are given in Gunter, Svennevig, and Wober, 1986, (p. 26).

The audience for radio news was much smaller, particularly for Radio 4 news. Since Radio 4 presented in-depth rather than popular coverage however, it should be compared with BBC's *Newsnight* and ITN's *Channel 4 News* news on television, which achieved similarly small audiences.

AUDIENCE VOLATILITY

How stable were these patterns of media use? Our panel provides more information about the stability of newspaper readership than programme listening since we have information on news-paper reading in our Mid-Term Wave as well as in later waves.

Over the winter of 1986–7 (that is, between the Mid-Term and Pre-Campaign Waves) well over two-thirds of newspaper readers stuck with the same paper. Among our fairly small sample, the *Sun* and the *The Times* fared worst, losing about a third of their original readers. *Sun* readers tended to switch to the *Mirror* and a variety of other papers; *Times* readers switched in large numbers to the newly established *Independent*. The *Guardian*, *Telegraph*, and *Mirror* did particularly well, retaining about four-fifths of their initial readers in each case. Only about half those who claimed to be regular paper readers in our Pre-Campaign Wave actually read a paper on the day on which they were interviewed during the final campaign, however.

MULTIPLE NEWS SOURCES

There is enough evidence of continuity here to suggest that it might be meaningful to classify a particular individual as a *'Guardian* reader' or an *'Express* reader'. But continuity alone is not enough to justify too much reliance on such a classification. People made use of multiple sources simultaneously. Relatively few claimed to read several daily papers regularly, but they read daily papers *and* Sunday papers *and* tuned in to radio and television.

The most popular Sunday paper amongst *Daily Express* readers was the *Sunday Express*; amongst *Daily Mail* readers, the *Mail on Sunday*; amongst *Daily Mirror* readers, the *Sunday Mirror*; amongst *Daily Telegraph* readers, the *Sunday Telegraph*; and amongst *Times* readers, the *Sunday Times*. Obvious enough, it might seem, but in every case except *The Times* less than half the daily paper's readers read the corresponding Sunday paper. So the most popular Sunday was not by any means an automatic or exclusive choice.

The *Star, Sun, Guardian,* and *Independent* did not have Sunday editions. For their readers, the Sunday choice was even less obvious. The favourite Sunday for *Sun* readers was its stable-mate the *News of the World*; but *Star* readers preferred the *People, Guardian* readers the *Observer,* and *Independent* readers (in our small sample, at least) preferred to take a day off from reading any paper at all on Sunday. Table 3.5 shows the overlap between each daily and that Sunday paper which was most popular amongst the daily's readers. For example, of all those who read either the daily *Sun* or the Sunday *News of the World* about

TABLE 3.5. *Overlap between Daily and Sunday Readership* (%)

Daily	% reading one or both who			Sunday
	read daily only	read both	read Sunday only	
Sun	33	32	35	News of the World
Mirror	50	30	20	Mirror
Mail	45	29	26	Mail
Guardian	31	28	41	Observer
Express	32	27	40	Express
The Times	4	23	73	The Times
Telegraph	58	20	22	Telegraph
Star	28	12	60	People

Notes: For each daily, the table shows the overlap with that Sunday which was most popular with the daily's readers in March 1987.

Figures are percentages of the total readership of the two papers (the daily and the Sunday) in question.

one-third read both, one-third read the *Sun* but not the *News of the World*, and one-third read the *News of the World* but not the *Sun*.

Judged by the percentage of readers in common between a daily and a Sunday, the overlap between *Guardian* and *Observer* or between *Sun* and *News of the World* was very similar to the overlap between daily and Sunday editions of the *Mirror, Mail,* and *Express*. Although substantial, this overlap never exceeded one-third of the joint readership of the daily and Sunday papers in question.

Different kinds of newspaper reader clearly had different tastes in radio and television news. Breakfast television, especially ITV's *TV-am* programme, seemed specially attractive to lowbrow paper readers: 32 per cent of lowbrow readers but only 5 per cent of highbrow readers regularly watched *TV-am*. In the early evening the BBC's *Six O'Clock News* did equally well amongst all categories of readers but ITV's shorter *News at 5.45* won 64 per cent of lowbrow readers but only 24 per cent of highbrow, and this carried forward into the regional news. Later in the evening the BBC's *Nine O'Clock News* proved substantially more attractive to highbrow readers than lowbrow, while the ITN's *News at Ten* was more attractive to lowbrow readers.

Low-audience in-depth news programmes on both channels— the BBC's *Newsnight* and ITV's *Channel 4 News*—won between three and four times as large an audience amongst highbrow readers as amongst lowbrow readers (in percentage terms, though not in absolute numbers). On the radio, the BBC's Radio 1 and Radio 2 news, like Commercial Radio news, got a somewhat larger audience amongst lowbrow readers while the BBC's Radio 4 news was eight times as popular with highbrow readers as with lowbrow. Indeed, the overlap between Radio 4's audience and highbrow press readership was as high as that between daily and Sunday editions of the same newspaper.

Regional news programmes appealed to the readers of regional newspapers: 25 per cent of *Glasgow Herald* readers and 43 per cent of *Scotsman* readers (based on our very small subsample) regularly listened to BBC Radio Scotland news.

Across the full range of programmes BBC news tended to appeal more to highbrow readers while ITV and Commercial Radio news tended to be more popular with lowbrow readers,

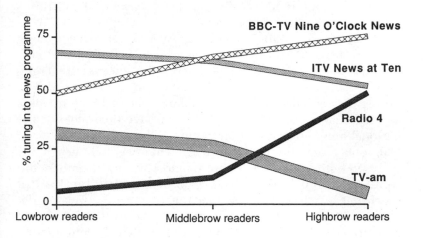

FIG. 3.1. Multiple Sources: The Viewing and Listening Habits of
Newspaper Readers (See Table 3.6)

TABLE 3.6. *How Newspaper Readers Used TV and Radio*

		% tuning into TV and radio news programmes among readers of		
		lowbrow papers	middlebrow papers	highbrow papers
Breakfast TV:	BBC	22	23	13
	ITV	32	26	5
Lunchtime TV:	BBC	26	27	19
	ITV	17	19	10
Early evening news:	BBC	63	64	62
	ITV	64	49	24
Main evening news:	BBC	50	66	75
	ITV	68	64	53
Regional TV news:	BBC	40	49	44
	ITV	43	42	20
Newsnight:	BBC	11	22	33
Channel 4 News:	ITV	5	9	20
Radio 4:	BBC	6	12	50
Radios 1 and 2:	BBC	48	42	37
Commercial Radio:	IBA	36	29	25

despite exceptions like ITV's *Channel 4 News* and the BBC's Radio 1 and Radio 2 news (Table 3.6).

Perhaps most striking was the large overlap between watching different television news programmes. On both BBC and ITV, regional news followed immediately after the early evening news. On both channels well over half the combined total audience for regional and national news regularly watched both national and regional news; about one-third restricted themselves to the national news and around one-tenth to the regional news.

It took more initiative to switch channels and watch the news on both BBC and ITV, but remarkably large numbers did so. Over a third of those who regularly watched breakfast or lunchtime television news claimed that they regularly watched it on *both* BBC and ITV. In the evening the overlap was even greater: over half of those who regularly watched evening news on television claimed that they regularly watched *both* BBC and ITV.

Fully 98 per cent of the whole electorate claimed that they regularly watched some television news, and 75 per cent claimed that they regularly watched *both* BBC and ITV (Table 3.7, Part 1). Of course, our question wording defined 'regularly' as 'three days a week'. So viewers could watch both BBC and ITV 'regularly' by alternating channels on alternate days. Many watched both BBC and ITV news on the same day however. During the final campaign when we asked whether people had watched BBC and ITV television news 'yesterday', 46 per cent of those who recalled watching TV news that day claimed they had watched *both* channels (Table 3.7, Part 2). This overlap between BBC and ITV viewing was so great, whether on every evening or over a few days, that we cannot reasonably categorize people into BBC viewers versus ITV viewers. We might conceivably distinguish between 'BBC only' and 'BBC plus ITV' viewers on a particular day during the campaign, but there were very few 'ITV only' news viewers on any campaign day. In terms of regular viewing over the course of a few days there were very few 'BBC only' news viewers either.

Many people seemed addicted to television news. Two-thirds regularly watched four or more television news programmes, almost half watched five or more, and over a quarter watched six or more (Table 3.8).

TABLE 3.7. *Overlapping Audiences for TV News*

	Source A	% of joint audience who regularly followed news on:			Source B
		Source A only	Sources A and B	Source B only	
PART 1: **'REGULAR' VIEWING**					
National and regional TV	BBC Six O'Clock	33	59	8	BBC Regional
	ITV at 5.45	31	54	15	ITV Regional
BBC and ITV	BBC breakfast and lunchtime	36	35	29	ITV breakfast and lunchtime
	BBC evening	25	55	20	ITV evening
	BBC any time	16	75	8	ITV any time
PART 2: **CAMPAIGN VIEWING**					
	BBC yesterday	40	46	15	ITV yesterday
	BBC today or yesterday	38	49	13	ITV today or yesterday

Notes: Part 1 based on Pre-Campaign Wave; Part 2 based on the average of the First Fortnight and Second Fortnight Waves.
   See notes to Table 3.4 for further details.

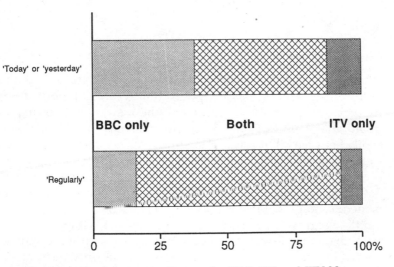

FIG. 3.2. Overlapping Audiences for BBC–TV and ITV News
(see Table 3.7)

TABLE 3.8. *TV News Addicts: Numbers of Television News Programmes Watched Regularly*

No. of programmes	%	Cumulative %
12	1	1
11	1	2
10	1	3
9	1	4
8	4	7
7	7	15
6	12	27
5	19	46
4	20	65
3	15	81
2	12	93
1	5	98
0	2	100

Notes: The twelve programmes were breakfast, lunch-time, early evening, main evening, and regional news on BBC and ITV, plus BBC's *Newsnight* and ITV's *Channel 4 News*.
   See also Table 3.16.

CHOICE OF MEDIA

Who read what? Who watched what? How far did social and political background factors, political interest, and motivations influence people's use of the media? The answer depends in part upon what aspect of media use concerns us—quantity of use, choice between highbrow and lowbrow sources, or choice between right-wing and left-wing sources. It proved relatively easy to predict whether people would choose highbrow or lowbrow news sources, but relatively difficult to predict any other aspect of media choice. Table 3.9 reports the results of a large number of multiple regression analyses. Only regressions which explained more than 10 per cent of the variation in media use are shown. There are remarkably few entries in the table since most of the regressions proved insignificant. So many media sources, or categories, attracted remarkably heterogeneous audiences.

TABLE 3.9. *Predictive Power of Multiple Regression Analyses of Media Use*

Media source	Wave	RSQ achieved using following:		
		Education Partisanship Age Ideology	plus: Interest	plus: Media motivations
Highbrow daily	MID	14	16	*
	PRE	13	16	17
	FF	14	15	*
	SF	11	*	*
Highbrow Sunday	PRE	14	16	*
BBC Radio 4	PRE	12	14	*
Right-wing daily	SF	11	*	*
Number of TV news programmes watched (out of 12)	PRE	8	10	12

Notes: Only regressions which explained more than 10 per cent of the variation in media use are shown. So all the media-use variables listed below but not shown in the table itself proved relatively unpredictable, i.e. they had heterogeneous audiences.

Regressions were used to predict reading, viewing, or listening to:

1. Highbrow daily paper; right-wing daily paper; reading no daily paper (in Mid-Term, Pre-Campaign, and Campaign Waves).
2. Highbrow Sunday paper: right-wing Sunday paper; reading no Sunday paper (in Pre-Campaign Wave).
3. BBC-TV news; ITV news; BBC-TV news but not ITV news; ITV news but not BBC-TV news; both BBC-TV and ITV news (in Pre-Campaign and Campaign Waves).
4. BBC Radios 1 and 2; BBC Radio 4; BBC and/or ITV breakfast TV news; BBC and/or ITV lunchtime TV news; BBC and/or ITV early evening TV news; BBC and/or ITV regional TV news; BBC and/or ITV main evening TV news; BBC *Newsnight* and/or ITV *Channel 4 News*; total number of TV news programmes watched regularly (in Pre-Campaign Wave).

An asterisk indicates that the additional predictors did not improve the predictive power of the multiple regression.

Who used highbrow sources?

Age, interest in politics, and above all, education encouraged the use of highbrow papers and BBC Radio 4. Highbrow television news (*Channel 4 News* and BBC's *Newsnight*) attracted a significantly more heterogeneous audience: age and political interest, *but not education*, encouraged use of highbrow television sources. Media-use motivations had surprisingly little influence on choice of highbrow or lowbrow sources (Table 3.10).

TABLE 3.10. *Multiple Regression Analyses of the Use of Highbrow News Sources (Pre-Campaign Wave)*

	Highbrow daily paper	BBC Radio 4	BBC *Newsnight/* ITV *Channel 4 News*
Education	33	27	5
Partisanship	0	−4	3
Age	12	23	15
On left	−1	2	0
On right	−1	2	5
Interest (MID)	*	14	17
Interest (PRE)	19	*	*
Guidance	−10	*	*
RSQ	17	14	7

Notes: Highbrow paper coded 2 for *Telegraph, Financial Times, Guardian, The Times, Independent, Observer*; zero for *Sun, Star, News of the World, People*. Other papers and none, coded 1.

Social background variables were forced into the regression; then interest variables, as measured in Mid-Term and Pre-Campaign Waves, were added stepwise provided they achieved 5 per cent significance; then the four motivation variables (reinforcement, guidance, information, and excitement), provided they achieved 5 per cent significance. An asterisk indicates a predictor was excluded because it did not achieve significance. Three of the motivation variables never achieved significance, and are not shown.

The influence of age, political interest, and education on highbrow paper reading varied little across successive waves of our survey, and was similar for Sunday and daily papers. Right

across the educational spectrum there was a general incre
highbrow media use with increasing education, but
quantum leap at degree level. Amongst those with univer
equivalent degrees about 60 per cent regularly read a highbrow
paper and 53 per cent regularly listened to BBC Radio 4. During
the final campaign about half these graduates had already read a
highbrow paper on the day we interviewed them and more of
them no doubt did so later in the evening (Table 3.11).

Very few of those who found politics uninteresting read a
highbrow paper. The more politically interested people were,
the more they read highbrow papers and listened to Radio 4. On
the raw figures in Table 3.11, older people seemed only a little

TABLE 3.11. *Trends in Highbrow Media Use by Education, Age, Political Interest, and Class*

	Read highbrow paper				Listened to BBC Radio 4 news PRE
	MID	PRE	FF	SF	
Education					
Degree	61	60	51	45	53
Professional qualification	17	25	13	15	28
A levels	21	29	18	22	24
O levels	10	15	7	8	15
CSEs	2	4	3	1	10
No qualification	5	6	3	4	12
Age					
Under 35	10	15	10	10	13
35–55	13	18	9	12	21
Over 55	16	18	17	16	28
Found politics (PRE)					
Very interesting	22	27	16	16	30
Fairly interesting	13	18	11	13	20
Not very interesting	4	8	5	8	9
Not at all interesting	3	3	2	0	9
Class					
Non-manual middle class	21	25	17	17	27
Manual working class	3	4	3	2	9

more likely to use highbrow sources than younger people, but the influence of age was masked by that of education. Older people were less well educated than younger people yet, despite that, they used highbrow news sources more than the young. So, allowing for differing education levels, the effect of age was quite strong as the multiple regression showed.

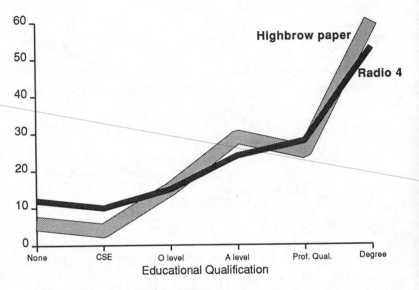

FIG. 3.3. Who Used Highbrow Sources? (see Table 3.11)

Who used right-wing sources?

The second most predictable aspect of media use was choice of a right-wing rather than an independent or left-wing paper. Not surprisingly the best predictor of reading a left- or right-wing paper was whether the readers themselves inclined to the left or right. In addition, education had a smaller and more variable influence, particularly on the choice of a right-wing Sunday paper (Table 3.12).

Readership of right-wing dailies increased steadily, all the way from left to right across our five-point self-assigned ideology scale. And whether judged by the percentage trends in Table 3.13 or by the changing regression coefficients in Table 3.12, the correlation between *readers' ideology* and their *papers' ideology*

TABLE 3.12. *Multiple Regression Analyses of Readership of Right-Wing Papers*

	Read right-wing daily				Read right-wing Sunday
	MID	PRE	FF	SF	PRE
Education	0	2	5	10	13
Partisanship	−1	−4	−1	−1	2
Age	−1	−1	0	3	2
On left	−17	−20	−16	−23	−7
On right	9	9	14	12	15
RSQ	6	7	7	11	5

Notes: Right-wing papers defined as *Express, Mail, Sun, Star, Telegraph, The Times, News of the World,* and coded 2; all other papers coded 0; no paper coded 1.

Political interest variables and motivations for media-use variables were included in stepwise regressions but proved insignificant. See notes to Table 3.10.

TABLE 3.13. *Trends in Right-Wing Media Use by Ideology and Class (%)*

	Read right-wing daily paper			
	MID	PRE	FF	SF
Ideology				
Left	27	21	16	12
Centre-left	39	35	24	18
Centre	49	43	28	32
Centre-right	60	57	44	43
Right	60	58	43	49
Class				
Non-manual middle class	52	50	38	36
Manual working class	47	42	28	29

Note: Voters' ideological classification based on their replies in the Pre-Campaign Wave.

increased towards the end of the campaign. In our Mid-Term Wave right-wingers were twice as likely to read a right-wing paper as left-wingers; but by the end of the election campaign right-wingers were not merely twice but four times as likely to do so. Clearly the increasing correlation between choice and personal ideology shown in Table 3.13 was *not* caused by the press influencing its readers. As we shall see in later chapters the press did influence its readers but, in Table 3.13, readers are classified once and once only by their ideology at a single point in time (the Pre-campaign Wave). The table therefore shows the changing reading habits of fixed subsets of voters, classified by their relative leftness or rightness at that single time-point. Thus it shows the influence of personal ideology on changing paper choices, not the reverse.

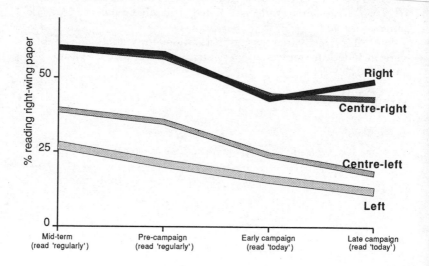

FIG. 3.4. Trends in Use of Right-Wing Sources by Voters' Ideology (see Table 3.13)

Significantly, class differences in right-wing or left-wing paper reading were slight: it was their ideology not their class that dictated people's choice of a left- or right-wing paper.

Who read anything at all?

Whether or not people read any paper at all proved generally fairly unpredictable, but during the closing stages of the campaign a pattern began to emerge. Older people were more likely to read a paper. So were those who sought information (rather than reinforcement, excitement, or guidance) from the media. Above all, strong partisans became particularly avid newspaper readers as election day approached (Table 3.14).

TABLE 3.14. *Multiple Regression Analyses of Newspaper Readership*

	MID	PRE	FF	SF
Education	1	−2	2	4
Partisanship	2	4	10	14
Age	1	3	9	7
On left	0	7	4	0
On right	1	7	5	4
Information	*	*	*	11
RSQ	0	1	2	4

Note: For the regression strategy see notes to Table 3.10.

In the mid-term, strong partisans were only about 5 per cent more likely to read a paper than weak partisans, but by the end of the campaign this gap had tripled (Table 3.15). At all times, those who found politics 'not at all interesting' were particularly unlikely to read a paper but few people fell into that extreme category.

Choice between alternative news programmes and channels

It was never very easy to predict who would watch BBC rather than ITV news or vice versa although there was a consistent but slight tendency for the better educated to prefer the BBC. It was much easier to predict people's total news viewing, their tendency to watch highbrow programmes like *Channel 4 News* and BBC's *Newsnight*, or their tendency to watch lunchtime television news.

TABLE 3.15. *Trends in Overall Readership by Partisanship and Political Interest* (%)

	Read any paper at all			
	MID	PRE	FF	SF
Partisanship				
Very strong party supporters	72	75	59	65
Fairly strong party supporters	78	77	62	63
Not very strong party supporters	71	70	52	53
Not party supporters at all	70	69	45	47
Political interest				
Very interested	76	74	58	57
Fairly interested	75	74	54	56
Not very interested	69	70	48	58
Not at all interested	64	66	45	39
Difference between readership rates of:				
Very interested and uninterested	12	8	13	18
Very strong party supporters and non-supporters	2	6	14	18

Notes: The figures show the percentage who read a paper 'regularly' in the Mid-Term and Pre-Campaign Waves, and who read a paper 'today' in the Campaign Waves. This change in question wording explains the sharp drop in all the figures between the Pre-Campaign and the Campaign Waves. The table cannot therefore be used to measure trends in raw readership rates, but it can be used to measure trends in the differences between readership rates in different subgroups.

Both partisan strength and political interest were measured in the Pre-Campaign Wave.

In short, channel choice was the least predictable aspect of television news viewing.

Age, interest in politics, strong partisanship, and a desire for guidance all encouraged high levels of news viewing, while education encouraged low levels (Table 3.16). Of the twelve main television news programmes, younger electors watched an average of 3.9 regularly, older electors 5.2. Those with a degree watched 3.6, while those with no educational qualification watched 4.8.

TABLE 3.16. *Multiple Regression Analyses: Who Were the TV News Addicts?*

	Number of TV news programmes watched
Education	−16
Partisanship	9
Age	16
On left	−7
On right	−7
Interest (MID)	19
Guidance	11
RSQ	12

Note: For the regression strategy, see notes to Table 3.10.

Since older people had fewer educational qualifications the influence of education and age overlapped, but each had an independent influence. Very strong partisans watched an average of 5.1 programmes while weak partisans watched about 4.0. Class and sex differences were small. The correlation between viewing rates and interest in politics in the Pre-Campaign Wave was also small, though viewing rates correlated more strongly with interest in politics in the Mid-Term and Campaign Waves (Table 3.17).

The highly educated tended to listen to BBC Radio 4 news and avoid breakfast, lunchtime, early evening, and regional television news. They were only slightly less likely than other people to listen to BBC Radios 1 and 2 or watch the main evening television news, and only slightly more likely to watch highbrow television news.

Older people also tended to listen to BBC Radio 4, but they were very much less likely to listen to Radios 1 and 2, and much more likely to watch lunchtime television and highbrow television.

Like the highly educated, those with a high level of interest in politics were particularly likely to listen to BBC Radio 4 and watch highbrow television news but, unlike the highly educated,

TABLE 3.17. *The Appetite for Television News by Education, Partisanship, and Age*

	Mean number of TV news programmes watched regularly
Education	
Degree	3.6
Professional qualification	4.2
A levels	4.1
O levels	4.2
CSEs	4.2
No qualification	4.8
Partisanship	
Very strong party supporters	5.1
Fairly strong party supporters	4.4
Not very strong party supporters	3.8
Not party supporters at all	4.2
Age	
Under 35	3.9
35–55	4.3
Over 55	5.2

they were also more likely than others to watch regional television news. Reinforcement seekers were a little more likely than others to watch the main evening television news (Table 3.18).

It would be misleading to focus too much attention on who watched BBC or ITV television news: most watched both. Any analysis of BBC news viewing, for example, is as much an analysis of news viewing in general as of BBC viewing in particular. BBC-TV's *unique* audience—that is, those who watched BBC-TV news but did not watch ITV news—was very difficult to predict, as was ITV's *unique* audience. There was a slight tendency for the highly educated to watch BBC-TV news and not ITV news, and a slight tendency for the relatively uneducated to do the opposite, but both patterns were weak. Political interest had no significant effect on which network people selected for exclusive viewing. Instead, political interest made people much more inclined to watch the news on *both* networks (Table 3.19).

TABLE 3.18. *Multiple Regression Analyses: Who Tuned in to Selected TV and Radio News Programmes?*

	Radio news		Television news					
	Radios 1 and 2	Radio 4	B	L	E	R	M	Channel 4/ Newsnight
Education	−6	27	−16	−16	−12	−13	−4	5
Partisanship	−2	−4	3	3	4	4	7	3
Age	−17	23	−4	20	4	5	5	15
On left	4	2	−2	−2	1	−7	6	0
On right	6	2	−3	−6	−8	−3	9	5
Interest (MID)	*	14	*	*	*	16	*	17
Reinforcement	*	*	*	*	*	*	11	*
RSQ	3	14	3	9	3	4	4	7

Notes: B = breakfast, L = lunch, E = early evening, R = regional, M = main evening news, irrespective of whether on BBC-TV or ITV, or both.
   For the regression strategy, see notes to Table 3.10.

Table 3.19. *Multiple Regression Analyses: Who Watched BBC Only, ITV Only, or Both BBC and ITV?*

	BBC only			ITV only			Both BBC and ITV		
	PRE	FF	SF	PRE	FF	SF	PRE	FF	SF
Education	10	8	5	−9	−11	−9	−6	−9	−1
Partisanship	−8	0	7	−4	4	3	11	−1	−3
Age	−2	−5	−2	−6	1	−9	4	10	8
On left	7	0	3	1	−7	−3	−6	1	−6
On right	8	3	6	1	−14	−4	−6	8	1
Interest (MID)	*	*	*	*	*	*	*	23	13
Interest (SF)	*	*	*	*	*	*	*	*	14
RSQ	2	1	1	1	2	1	2	8	5

Note: For the regression strategy, see notes to Table 3.10.

As the campaign advanced, the difference between the viewing habits of the politically interested and uninterested widened sharply. Our Pre-Campaign Wave showed that almost everyone, irrespective of their degree of interest in politics, claimed that they regularly watched television news, either on BBC or on ITV.

Around three-quarters claimed that they regularly watched television news on both and the difference between the politically
interested and uninterested was small: 77 per cent of the most
interested watched the news on both channels, but so did 69 per
cent of the least interested—a difference of only 8 per cent. But
the difference between the chances of the most interested and
the least interested viewing the news on both channels rose from
8 per cent in the Pre-Campaign Wave to 17 per cent in the first
half of the campaign and then to 23 per cent in the second half.

Naturally, fewer people watched television news on any one
day than watched it 'regularly' (defined as at least three days
a week). So the big drop in viewing rates between the Pre-
Campaign and Campaign Waves is partly (though not completely)
due to changes in question wording. But even within the campaign, when the question remained unchanged, viewing rates
declined amongst those who found politics relatively uninteresting
while they remained stable amongst those who found politics
interesting. Thus the steadily increasing difference between the
viewing rates of the politically interested and uninterested owed
more to the uninterested switching off than to the interested
switching on. That finding might disappoint the parties but it
would not surprise them (Table 3.20).

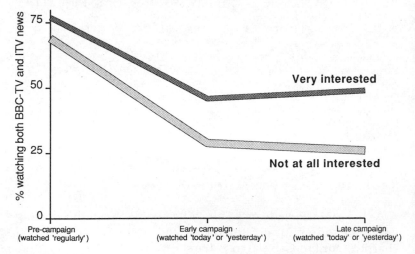

FIG. 3.5. Trends in Watching TV News by Voters' Political Interest (see
Table 3.20)

TABLE 3.20. *Trends in Watching Television News by Political Interest* (%)

	BBC only			ITV only			BBC *and* ITV			BBC *or* ITV		
	PRE	FF	SF	PRE	FF	SF	PRE	FF	SF	PRE	FF	SF
Political interest												
Very interested	90	77	76	35	55	58	77	46	49	98	85	85
Fairly interested	93	68	69	80	49	48	74	40	39	99	77	79
Not very interested	84	64	60	81	43	40	68	33	30	97	74	69
Not at all interested	83	54	52	81	47	39	69	29	26	96	71	65
Difference	7	23	24	4	8	19	8	17	23	2	14	20

Notes: In the Pre-Campaign Wave, the figures refer to those who watched any news programme 'regularly', i.e. at least three times a week. In the Campaign Waves, the figures refer to those who watched the news 'today' or 'yesterday'. This change in question wording explains the major drop in viewing rates between the Pre-Campaign and Campaign Waves.

Political interest was measured at the time of the interview.

Difference = difference between viewing rates of the very interested and the completely uninterested.

CONCLUSIONS

Reading highbrow newspapers and listening to highbrow radio news programmes correlated strongly with age, interest in politics, and education, but highbrow television news attracted a much wider and more heterogeneous audience. The audience for highbrow television was influenced by age and political interest but *not* by education.

Readers' own ideology influenced their choice between right-wing and left-wing papers. The correlation between readers' own ideology and their papers' ideology increased towards the end of the campaign as those on the left became much more reluctant to continue reading right-wing papers. Class had little influence: it was ideology not class that influenced people's choice between left- and right-wing papers.

Overall, media-use motivations had surprisingly little influence on media choice, though guidance seekers watched television more and read highbrow papers less.

But the most striking feature of the public's news gathering was their use of multiple sources. Half the readers of highbrow papers regularly listened to BBC Radio 4 News, a third regularly watched BBC's *Newsnight*, and three-quarters regularly watched the BBC's *Nine O'Clock News*.

More significantly, for our understanding of the non-intellectual bulk of the electorate, there was a huge overlap between viewing the news on BBC-TV and ITV, which has important implications for media influence. Few people read more than one national daily paper but most regularly watched several TV news programmes and, in particular, most regularly watched *both* BBC and ITV News. During the campaign itself, almost half the television news audience watched both BBC and ITV news on the same day. So, if news media do have any political influence, readers of different papers could be influenced in different directions depending upon the content of their own particular papers; but BBC and ITV viewers could not be influenced in different directions, even if the content of BBC and ITV were different, because the two television news organizations very largely share the same audience. In so far as there was a difference, ITV's news audience was a subset of the BBC's. As we shall see in a later chapter, the contents of BBC-TV and ITV news were remarkably similar, unlike the contents of different newspapers, which makes it even less profitable to look for divergent political trends between BBC and ITV viewers.

That does not mean that television news has no potential for influence. Quite the contrary. Because it reaches so many citizens, television's potential for influence is considerable. But while newspaper influence can reveal itself in differential effects, television influence is more likely to reveal itself in consensual effects. Newspaper content might cause divergent political trends in different subsections of the electorate (readers of different papers), while television coverage would be more likely to cause homogeneous, consensual trends that would apply throughout the whole electorate. We shall return to this theme in later chapters.

4

National and International News on Television

Since the 1960s British voters have quoted television as their main source of news about politics; before that they quoted newspapers (Harrop, 1987, p. 53; IBA, 1987, p. 17). It is a world-wide phenomenon: Americans also switched from newspapers to television as their prime source of news at the start of the 1960s (*American Enterprise*, 1990, p. 95), and now that they have competitive elections and public opinion polls, Soviet citizens also quote television as their main source of election news (White, 1990, p. 53). In Britain, reliance on television news increased, and reliance on newspapers decreased, during the 1980s (Negrine, 1989, p. 1). 'Modern election campaigns have to a considerable extent become fully and truly television campaigns' (Blumler, Gurevitch, and Ives, 1978).

We asked our panel about their reliance upon several sources: television generally, BBC-TV news, ITV news, Party Election Broadcasts, BBC radio news, Commercial radio news, newspapers, party leaflets, and conversations with family and friends. The two sources used by almost all members of our panel were television news and personal conversations. Somewhat fewer used newspapers and a lot less used radio. We have no direct evidence about the content of private conversations though anecdotal evidence suggests that they are often prompted by what people have read, heard, or seen in the mass media.

Mass-circulation British newspapers are, and always have been, politically committed journals of opinion rather than purely objective journals of record. There is a debate about the alleged 'depoliticization' of the British press in recent years but that concerns a change of emphasis in the tabloid press from hard political news to entertainment and 'human interest' stories (see Negrine, 1989, ch. 4). There is still no doubt about the political and even *party*-political line taken by most newspapers at most times (see Chapter 3, Table 1). At election times most papers issue explicit endorsements, though their general news coverage is so heavily slanted that explicit statements of their political preferences are redundant. Of the eleven national dailies published at the time of the 1987 election, seven explicitly called for a Conservative victory and only two called for a Labour victory (the *Mirror* and the *Guardian*—though the *Guardian* also has a history of sympathy for the Liberals and did not call for a Labour victory in 1983). The new and low-circulation tabloid, *Today*, called for a coalition government. The *Independent* refused to issue an endorsement: it was the only newspaper whose chief selling point was its political independence, and it sold less than 300,000 copies to an electorate of over 43 million (Harrop, 1988; MacArthur, 1989; British press bias on social and political issues of a less overtly party-political nature is discussed in Hollingsworth, 1986; Newton, 1988b).

British television, on the other hand, is committed to balanced and impartial broadcasting. As Seaton and Pimlott note: 'Balance in broadcasting is a strange concept with no equivalent for the press. The assumption in the case of newspapers is of imbalance with each paper reflecting a particular editorial or proprietorial point of view' (Seaton and Pimlott, 1987a, p. 133). Although the concept of balance in political broadcasting is complex, the practice is simple. In theory balance might mean objectivity, that is, an accurate reflection of the real world, and an accurate reflection would have to be a representative selection, since all the truth about a day in the life of the world cannot be packed into a thirty-minute news bulletin. Philosophers might argue that such objectivity could not exist and even news editors might occasionally doubt their own ability to supply it. But, in practice, balance is quite the opposite of objectivity. It means treating the major political forces in the country with some degree of equality. The exact formula has been adjusted from time to time in response to changes in party support. Seaton and Pimlott (1987a) present a fascinating account of the historical development of 'balance' in British broadcasting. Its origins lie in the political bargain struck by the parties under the wartime coalition government. Its purpose was, and is, to avoid a major political fight for the control of broadcasting by 'sharing out the spoils'. As the weight of different political parties changes, this is reflected in changing access to radio and television. Balance is defined, and redefined, by an informal inter-party committee. In 1987, for the first time since the early 1950s, it was defined as exact equality for each of the three party groups: Conservative, Labour and Alliance (Butler, 1989, pp. 97–9; in 1951 the three parties got equal time on television, but not on radio which had a larger audience at that time).

Technically, the inter-party committee merely recommends the ratios of free advertising time (the so-called 'PEBs' or Party Election Broadcasts) to be offered to the different parties. But informally these party-agreed ratios are accepted by the news broadcasters, and applied to their own news bulletins as well as to PEBs. In 1987 they applied the ratio not only to the amount of news bulletin time notionally attributed to each party, but even to the number of lead stories associated with each party. So if a bulletin led with a story about the Conservatives on one day, the news editors would try to lead off with a story about Labour on the second day and a story about the Alliance on the third day (Axford and Madgwick, 1989, p. 149).

News editors might feel that the actions, policies or prospects of one party are much more newsworthy than those of another but they are constrained to give them equal time and equal billing. Balance means giving equal time to the dull and the sensational, the radical and the traditional, the important and the unimportant, the front-runners and the also-rans. In 1987 the Alliance were delighted to win the right to so much exposure, though they soon found that it imposed a heavy burden on the party to fill the available time without becoming dangerously overexposed. Viewers are under no obligation to tolerate the dull, the unimportant, the politician without a message. Balance, as interpreted by the broadcasters, can be a mixed blessing for all concerned.

In fact, equal time guarantees neither objectivity nor balance. Equal time does not guarantee equal treatment. Media specialists always emphasize the significance of the short, catchy 'sound bite' that encapsulates a political message. A politician who can make his point in thirty seconds is likely to be more effective than one who takes five minutes. It may be better to list two faults in your opponent's policy than merely one, but it is a mistake to try to list a dozen. On television, impact is often inversely related to length. For that reason British parties sometimes shorten their permitted PEBs in order to sharpen their message, effectively rejecting free television advertising time! (British PEBs are typically more than twenty times as long as an American party's political advert. British parties have always wanted more, shorter PEBs rather than fewer, longer ones, but the broadcasters have resisted these demands.)

Moreover, it is totally misleading to measure the impact of a story by its length rather than its content. As Pilsworth (1986) says: 'The dogged defence of the stop-watch as arbiter of impartiality should be allowed to lapse . . . no-one can seriously argue that genuine balance and impartiality can be ascertained in this way.' Under the formula for calculating balance in British political television, a five-minute argument between Alliance leaders David Owen and David Steel would count as five minutes' coverage of the Alliance. Two minutes of Thatcher accusing Labour of being unpatriotic would count as two minutes' coverage of the Conservatives. Ten minutes of Kinnock trying to explain the impenetrable subtleties of his defence policy (which he himself abandoned after the election) would count as ten minutes' coverage of Labour. Clearly, some of this coverage would help the party covered and some would not. In particular, the rules of balance take no account of the policy issue being discussed. Ten minutes asking a politician questions about a policy he wishes to highlight count the same as ten minutes forcing him to discuss an issue he would far rather forget.

None the less equal time conveys a message to the viewer. It suggests that television is at least trying to be impartial. It underlines the claim of television to be above the party battle, whatever it may do for the parties themselves. So, as we shall see in later chapters, it tends to make the viewer accept that television is truly balanced and (what is rather different) truly unbiased. It adds to the authority and legitimacy of television news, which is already inflated by the misperception that 'the camera cannot lie'.

In order to assess the content of television news, we shall not try to compare it with some alternative and more authoritative 'reality'. Others, notably the Glasgow University Media Group (1976, 1980, 1982), have tried that approach but it is difficult to find a more authoritative source. Instead we shall simply measure the components, the balance, within the media content itself;

then measure the trends in that content; and relate it to the electorate's own (admittedly subjective) perspective on political debate.

We analysed television news during the same weeks as our Pre-Campaign and Campaign Waves of interviews. Although we recorded and analysed various other television news programmes, this chapter is based upon our analysis of the four national news programmes with the largest viewing audiences: the BBC's *Six O'Clock News* and *Nine O'Clock News* and ITV's *News at 5.45* and *News at Ten*. This gives a direct objective measure of the main mass media source that people relied upon during the campaign. In this chapter we look at these programmes' collective content. In the next chapter we shall distinguish between them, and also between national and regional news programmes.

How was the electoral contest presented? Positively or negatively? Were parties shown presenting their own case or attacking their opponents? Were parties presented as monolithic unities or as collections of factions and individuals with differing viewpoints? Did the broadcasters attempt to guide viewers' interpretation of news events? Did the parties receive balanced coverage—whatever balance may mean? Did television present a particular agenda of issues? Did that agenda reflect the agenda of one party more than others?

HOW TELEVISION NEWS PRESENTED POLITICAL CONTROVERSY

We analysed all headlines and stories that appeared on the four main national television news bulletins during our pre-campaign week and the final campaign, a total of 2,232 items altogether (Table 4.1). We categorized and coded a dozen different aspects of each item. In particular we noted whether the item had any overt relevance to the party battles of the election campaign or whether it seemed to be about non-election news. Those items which were overtly relevant to the party battle were categorized as:

1. Simple presentation (that is, one party was allowed to state its own case),

TABLE 4.1. *Total Numbers of Headlines and Stories Analysed*

	Pre-campaign Wave (March 1987)	Final campaign (May–June 1987)	TOTAL
ITV *News at 5.45*	60	347	407
BBC *Six O'Clock News*	86	550	636
BBC *Nine O'Clock News*	82	524	606
ITV *News at Ten*	81	502	583
TOTAL	309	1,923	2,232

2. Controversy (that is, one party attacked another, defended itself against attack, or joined in a multi-party controversy), or
3. Review (that is, television journalists presented an 'independent' review of some aspect of the campaign—policies, issues, leaders, localities, etc.).

Over the whole period of our analysis almost exactly half the television news items were about apparently non-election or background news. (We shall question that appearance later.) A very few were review items, and just under a quarter each were simple presentation and controversy items.

There were large differences between one week and another. For our television news content analysis we shall divide the final campaign up into five 'weeks' (though the first and last are not full calendar weeks) and look at trends across these six 'weeks': our pre-campaign week in March plus the five weeks (or part weeks) of the final campaign (Table 4.2).

The same trends as regards the amount of controversy show up in analyses of news stories and news headlines, but the trends were sharper and more extreme with news headlines. In the pre-campaign week, only 36 per cent of news headlines were classified as election news. Election news took a larger share of the headlines when the final campaign got into its stride: its share rose to 39 per cent in the first week of the final campaign, 50 per cent in the second, and 57 per cent in the third before sinking back to around 50 per cent in the last two weeks of the campaign.

Controversy reached a peak in the third week of the campaign. In March, and for the first two weeks of the final campaign, there

TABLE 4.2. *Trends in Simple Presentation, Controversy, and Non-Election News on Television (headlines only) (%)*

	Pre-campaign week	Final campaign				
	30 Mar.–3 Apr.	12–15 May Week 1	18–22 May Week 2	25–9 May Week 3	1–5 June Week 4	8–10 June Week 5
Background news	64	61	50	43	51	49
Election news						
Presentation	27	24	32	17	26	35
Controversy	9	14	18	41	23	16
Total	36	39	50	57	49	51

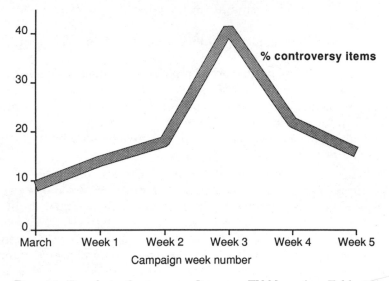

FIG. 4.1. Trends in Controversy Items on TV News (see Table 4.2)

was at least twice as much simple party presentation as controversy, but in the third week there was well over twice as much
controversy as presentation. Then in the last two weeks presentation again exceeded controversy and to an increasing extent;
so by the end of the campaign, there was once again more than
twice as much presentation as controversy. On television at least,
the campaign very clearly reached a climax in the third week
(that is, 25–9 May).

HOW TELEVISION NEWS DEFINED THE POLITICAL AGENDA

We coded the main issue in every headline and story on television
news. If a story dealt equally with several issues, or dealt with
none, we coded it as having no clear issue focus. We used a total
of sixty-seven highly specific issue categories, grouped into ten
broader categories:

1. unfocused (no issue/multi-issue)
2. leadership
3. philosophy
4. economy
5. physical security (including defence, terrorism, and crime)

6. social security (including health, education, welfare, and the environment)
7. two nations (geographically, socially, or racially defined divisions in British society)
8. special interests (unions, employers, women, agriculture, etc.)
9. campaign progress (poll results, arguments over tactical voting, coalition deals, etc.)
10. non-political topics (sport, medicine, royalty, showbiz, human interest, etc.)

The percentage of items falling into these different categories defines a particular *media agenda*. We can calculate numerous media agendas: agendas on different channels; agendas at different times; headline agendas and story agendas; election news agendas and non-election news agendas. An important distinction is that between overtly *election campaign news* and non-election, or what might be called *background news*—those items that at least on the surface seem to have no obvious connection with the election result. Many items of foreign news fall into the category of background news. Often, news analysts restrict their study to overtly election news items (and define even these in a very restrictive fashion) but it is very revealing to analyse complete news bulletins in full.

Background news provides the most immediate context in which election news is viewed by the electorate. Suppose, for example, that an election news item focusing on a Labour Party call for cuts in defence expenditure is followed by an item about an American warship destroyed by an Iraqi Exocet missile, or a report on the French trial of a Nazi war criminal. (Both these stories ran for several days during the final campaign.) Although these background items have no direct, obvious logical connection with the British election campaign, the viewer then sees a call for British defence cuts against background news that underlines the fact that we live in a dangerous world full of violent men. There is an emotional, and ultimately even a logical, connection between such background news and the election item.

So there are two questions:

1. What was television's *election agenda*, that is, the pattern of issues covered in election campaign news items?

2. What was television's *background agenda*, that is, the pattern of issues covered in the rest of the news?

About a quarter of all the election news items had no clear issue focus—they tended to be 'campaign trail' items or even manifesto reports that touched on many issues but failed to focus on one in particular (Table 4.3). One-fifth focused on physical security issues, about one-tenth on the economy, and another tenth on social security. One-third of background news items had no relevance to any current issue in British politics but almost half of all background items focused on physical security. These were items about defence, war, riot, rebellion, terrorism, and crime in other places with no overt link to Britain. None the less these were items that focused upon topics which were relevant to British politics. 'A quarrel in a faraway country between people of whom we know nothing' may not seem relevant to the politics of British defence but, as Neville Chamberlain later found out, war anywhere *is* relevant to our defence policies.

TABLE 4.3. *Television's Election News and Background News Agendas during the Final Campaign* (%)

	Election news	Background news
Unfocused	25	1
Leadership	6	0
Philosophy	7	2
Economy	12	9
Physical security	20	48
Social security	10	1
Two nations	4	0
Special interests	2	1
Campaign progress*	15	3
Non-political topics	0	37

* Some aspects of the campaign, including the technical arrangements of the returning officers, for example, were classified as non-partisan and therefore background news.

There were sharp trends and week-to-week variations in the television news agenda but these were confined to election news items; the pattern of issues covered in background news items remained remarkably stable—as might be expected, given that the background news was not driven by the dynamics of the British election campaign.

The election news agenda

First, let us look at overtly *election news* items (Table 4.4). Unfocused, no-issue, or multi-issue items simply did not appear on any programme in the pre-campaign week, but in the first week of the final campaign they comprised 43 per cent of all election news. That percentage dropped sharply and continuously until it bottomed out at 12 per cent in the fourth week before shooting up again to 35 per cent in the fifth and final week. So the viewers got a large helping of muddy, unfocused reporting at the start and end of the final campaign.

TABLE 4.4. *A Moving Consensus on the Issues in Election News Items (headlines and stories)* (%)

	Pre-campaign week	Final campaign				
		Week 1	Week 2	Week 3	Week 4	Week 5
Unfocused	0	43	30	16	12	35
Economic and social	25	10	26	25	23	18
Physical security	69	13	13	37	21	11
Campaign progress	3	11	10	11	23	18

Overall, 15 per cent of television news in the final campaign focused upon non-substantive issues associated with the campaign itself—primarily assessment of how well each of the parties was doing, how large a lead the Conservatives had over Labour, whether the Alliance challenge was fading, and the like. In March these campaign progress items made up only 3 per cent of election news and for the first three weeks of the final campaign only 11 per cent. But in the fourth week almost a quarter of all election news was about the state of the parties, and the prospects (or lack of them) for a hung parliament. In the fifth week the focus on campaign progress dropped back slightly from 23 per cent to 18 per cent as it became clear that there would be no significant late swing towards Labour or the Alliance.

Items about economic, social, and (physical) security affairs made up 42 per cent of election news during the final campaign—two-thirds of all the items that focused upon specific substantive issues. We can usefully group economic and social affairs together (22 per cent) and contrast the trends in coverage of these issues with the trends in coverage of security issues (20 per cent).

Apart from the first and last weeks of the final campaign, when the news was so dominated by unfocused items, economic and social affairs received remarkably steady coverage: in March, and throughout most of the final campaign, coverage ranged between 23 per cent and 26 per cent of each week's election news. The balance between economic and social affairs shifted slightly from time to time, but overall coverage remained almost invariant.

But coverage of security issues (that is, defence plus law and order) varied dramatically. In March, when Thatcher was in Moscow, 69 per cent of all election news was about security. At the start of the final campaign coverage dropped to 13 per cent and stayed there for two weeks. Then, in the controversial third week, it tripled to 37 per cent before dropping to 21 per cent in the fourth and 11 per cent in the fifth. So economic and social issues got much the same coverage as security issues in the first week of the final campaign, and more in the second, fourth, and fifth weeks, but far less in the third week (and very much less still in the pre-campaign week).

The background news agenda

While election news coverage varied dramatically, reflecting the cut and thrust of party debate, background news did not (Table 4.5). Economic and social issues never got more than 12 per cent nor less than 9 per cent of coverage at any time before or during the final campaign. Similarly, security issues never got less than 42 per cent nor more than 54 per cent. Background news was always dominated by security issues.

The people's agenda

How did television's news agenda compare with the electorate's? We asked our panel: 'What seems the main issue being stressed by each of the parties at the moment? And what do you yourself

TABLE 4.5. *A Stable Consensus on the Issues in Background News Items (headlines and stories)* (%)

	Pre-campaign week	Final campaign				
		Week 1	Week 2	Week 3	Week 4	Week 5
Unfocused	0	1	1	1	1	2
Economic and social	11	10	9	9	11	12
Physical security	42	49	51	43	45	54
Campaign progress	0	6	1	4	2	3
Non-political	47	33	36	42	40	30

think is the main issue that the parties should be talking about?' In addition we asked our panel to tell us 'how important to you in making up your mind how to vote is the unemployment issue, the inflation issue, the defence issue, and health, education, and social service issues?' The first set of questions tells us about the electorate's priorities, and their perceptions of party priorities. The second set of questions provides us with alternative measures of the importance the electorate attached to a variety of specific issues. Alternative measures are useful because issue salience is a subtle and elusive concept: people may feel the parties should be talking about an important problem (perhaps in some moral sense) yet base their own voting choice upon other issues.

During the final campaign television stressed security issues as much as economic and social issues in its election coverage, and focused overwhelmingly upon security issues in its background news, as we have just seen. The public thought the Conservative Party stressed both equally, and that Labour and the Alliance stressed economic and social affairs much more than security. When they were asked what the parties 'should be' talking about people opted overwhelmingly for economic and social affairs. Even Labour seemed to focus less upon these issues than the public wanted. When they were asked directly about the importance of four specific issue areas for their voting choice, electors attributed the greatest influence to 'health, education, and social issues' and the least to 'defence'.

Overall, therefore, the agenda set by television was miles away from the agenda of issues that the electorate rated important and wanted discussed (Table 4.6). Television's election news agenda

TABLE 4.6. *Rival Issue Agendas during the Final Campaign: Parties',*
People's, and Television's (%)

	Economic and social issues	Security issues	No focus/ DK, non-political
Television			
Election items	22	20	25
Background news	10	48	38
Parties (as perceived by panel)			
Conservative	38	33	21
Labour	68	13	14
Alliance	40	12	38
People			
Main issue that should be discussed	83	11	4
Issue is 'extremely important' for vote:*			
— Inflation	44		
— Unemployment	64		
— Health, education, social service	77		
— Defence	49		

* Figures based upon four questions which asked for the importance attached to
each of the four issues.

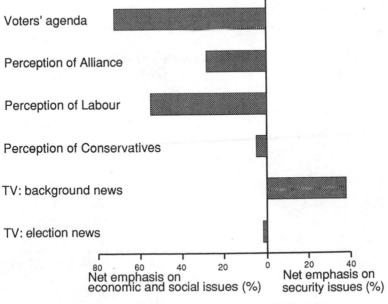

FIG. 4.2. Rival Issue Agendas (see Table 4.6)

was biased towards security issues when compared with the electorate's own agenda; and television's background news agenda extremely so. (For evidence that British journalists are more willing than their American counterparts to accept the issue agenda laid down by the parties see Weaver, Wilhoit, and Semetko, 1986, though their study is based upon an analysis of the press rather than television.)

TABLE 4.7. *Trends in the TV Agenda* (%)

	Pre-campaign week	Final campaign				
		Week 1	Week 2	Week 3	Week 4	Week 5
Unemployment	3	4	12	3	9	1
Inflation	0	0	1	1	0	1
Defence	35	5	12	26	3	3
Health education social service	6	3	13	14	10	6

Note: Figures are percentages of television's 'election news' items.

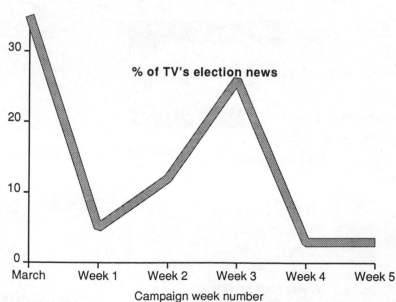

FIG. 4.3. TV's Emphasis on Defence Issues (see Table 4.7)

HOW TELEVISION NEWS TREATED THE PARTIES

How did television treat the parties? What were the party implications of television's handling of political controversy and the issue agenda? How did television present party leaders? Did it imply party unity (or disunity)? And how did television journalists guide viewers' interpretation of the news?

There ought to be a simple and agreed measure of the amount of coverage given to each party. Before the campaign opened, the parties agreed between themselves that they should get equal numbers of PEBs (Party Election Broadcasts) and news editors took that as a guide to the amount of news coverage that should be devoted to each of the parties. Harrison presents figures showing that the Conservative Party, Labour Party, and Alliance each got 32 per cent of radio and television news coverage during the final campaign, and other parties 4 per cent, with very little variation across channels (Harrison, 1988, p. 143). So it would appear that the major parties did indeed get the promised equal treatment.

According to Axford and Madgwick parity also extended even to 'their placement in the running order, the number and style of leader profiles and so on, right down to the reporting of gaffes made while on the stump' (Axford and Madgwick, 1989, p. 149) That claim underlines the general conclusion that television clung to the concept of balance even at the expense of news values.

But it all depends on how you compute balance. In particular it depends crucially on what items are counted as election news and what items are disregarded. If we take a more comprehensive look at television news bulletins, and avoid arbitrary exclusions, it is clear that television news was not in fact balanced in its coverage of the parties.

Party and government shares of news coverage

Apart from a few review items, election news items divide into two broad groups, *presentation* and *controversy*, each of which comprised over two-fifths of election news items. Presentation items usually focused upon just one party, presenting its case in some way. Controversy items usually included two or more parties, though they occasionally focused on a single party launching an attack on others (without a reply within that same news item), committing a gaffe or indiscretion, or responding to a chorus of criticism from journalists.

When we categorized news items as presentation or controversy items we also noted what kind of presentation or controversy occurred and which party or parties were involved. We must stress that our classification of the parties involved in a news item was not based upon mere token appearances. For example, all the main parties might briefly appear in an item but after viewing the video recording we might decide that the main point of the item was a clash between Conservative and Labour. Especially in election campaigns, journalists may include token appearances merely to satisfy some arithmetical criterion of balance (in the sense of time coverage or numbers of appearances) but we tried to categorize the news item by its main point, by how it might appear to a typically none-too-attentive viewer.

A mere 4 per cent of *presentation* items involved pairs of parties; 78 per cent involved a single party and 12 per cent all three main parties. These single-party presentation items were very heavily biased towards the Conservative government, which got almost three times as much coverage as Labour and well over twice as much as the Alliance. *As a party*, the Conservatives got 23 per cent of the coverage compared with 18 per cent for the Alliance and 16 per cent for Labour (Table 4.8). But in addition, *as a government*, the Conservatives got another 21 per cent of the coverage. Now it is true that the items we classified as 'government in action' contained no explicit reference to the election. But an item presenting Geoffrey Howe as a strong Foreign Secretary successfully forcing the Iranians to release a British diplomat was as helpful to his party's re-election campaign as any explicit statement of policy. Most 'government in action' items seemed to enhance the government's image as tough and decisive. While coverage is not necessarily helpful coverage—for any party—and events outside government control may lead to unfavourable publicity for the government, it would be extremely naïve to suppose that leading government politicians are unaware of their ability to generate favourable news coverage by taking initiatives, or by choosing to act in a more public way where

TABLE 4.8. *How the Parties were Covered during the Final Campaign* (%)

	Presentation items	Controversy items
Government in action	21	2
Conservative only	23	8
Labour only	16	7
Alliance only	18	6
Total for single parties (or govt)	78	21
Conservative and Labour	3	37
Conservative and Alliance	1	10
Labour and Alliance	0	8
Total for pairs of parties	4	55
Conservative, Labour, and Alliance	12	21

Note: The remaining items involved the Scottish and Welsh Nationalists, Northern Irish parties, and others.

publicity is likely to be favourable and in a less public way where publicity is likely to be adverse.

Party coverage in *controversy* items was very different: 76 per cent involved two or three parties and a mere 2 per cent involved 'government in action'. Single-party items of a controversial nature totalled 21 per cent and focused about equally on Conservative, Labour, and the Alliance. But controversy items, just like presentation items, did not treat the parties equally. Just over half of them focused on a *pair* of parties: 37 per cent on Conservative versus Labour, 10 per cent on Conservative versus the Alliance, and 8 per cent on Labour versus the Alliance. (There were, of course, many three-way controversy items as well.) So the Conservative versus Labour battle got four times as much coverage as any other battle between a pair of parties. While presentation items focused heavily on the government, controversy items focused heavily on the Conservative versus Labour battle. Both the opposition parties were disadvantaged in *presentation* items while the Alliance was marginalized in *controversy* items.

Trends in party coverage

In one form or another the bias in presentation items towards the Conservative government existed throughout the campaign. It increased towards the end as 'government in action' items became the most frequent form of non-controversial political news. But bias during the final campaign never came anywhere near the degree of bias in the pre-campaign week when 85 per cent of presentation items concerned 'government in action'—mainly, but not exclusively, about Thatcher's photogenic trip to Moscow. During the final campaign, 'government in action' items never exceeded 37 per cent in any one week. Even that gave the Conservative government five times as much single-party non-controversial coverage as Labour in the last two weeks of the campaign.

Television's treatment of party controversy also changed towards the end of the campaign. For the first three weeks a fairly steady 30 per cent of controversy items focused on Conservative versus Labour battles; but in the fourth week this rose to 51 per cent and fell back only as far as 44 per cent in the final week.

Both elements of party bias therefore—uncontroversial coverage of 'government in action', and concentration on the Conservative versus Labour two-party battle—became more pronounced towards the end of the campaign (Table 4.9).

Issue agendas and parties

Budge and Farlie (1983) have argued that a media focus on security issues in an election will almost always help right-wing parties and hurt left-wing parties, no matter the country or the date of the election. Security issues are 'naturally right-wing' issues; conversely, social and economic issues are 'naturally left wing' issues, according to Budge and Farlie. If they are correct then we can now restate our findings about issue agendas in left–right terms and hence in party terms.

The electorate's own agenda was the most 'naturally left-wing', followed by Labour's and the Alliance's. The Conservative Party agenda was only very moderately right-wing. The election news agenda was roughly balanced in the first, fourth, and fifth

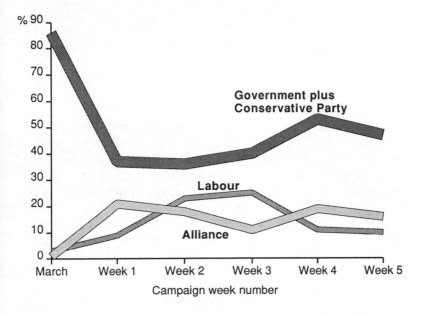

FIG. 4.4. Party Presentation on TV News (see Table 4.9)

TABLE 4.9. *Trends in Party Coverage* (%)

	Pre-campaign week	Final campaign				
		Week 1	Week 2	Week 3	Week 4	Week 5
Presentation items						
Govt in action	85	11	6	24	37	27
Conservatives only	1	26	30	16	16	20
Labour only	3	9	23	25	11	10
Alliance only	1	21	18	11	19	16
Controversy items						
Con v. Lab	35	28	33	29	51	44
Con v All	4	0	20	2	14	7
Lab v All	8	17	0	12	8	3

Note: Only selected patterns of party coverage are shown here. For the full range, see Table 4.8.

weeks, biased towards the left in the second week, and towards
the right in the third week. Background news on television was
overwhelmingly right-wing in its subtle and unarticulated implications.

Leader quality

Politicians state their policies, explicitly, in speeches. But they
also state their case, implicitly, in planned and occasionally
unplanned photo-opportunities. We counted the number of
times each party leader was shown on television news displaying a
personal quality by means of a photo-opportunity: showing they
'cared' by having a chat with a hospital patient, showing they
were 'unwilling to listen' by interrupting a questioner, and so on
(Table 4.10). Obviously, for this kind of measurement we had to
specify clearly and in advance just what kinds of action we would
classify as 'caring', 'decisive', or 'willing to listen'.

We also counted the number of times television journalists
made 'contextualizing' remarks about party leaders, emphasizing

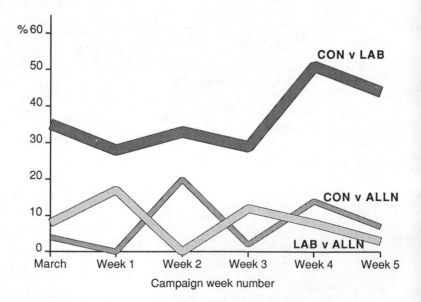

FIG. 4.5. Types of Controversy on TV News (see Table 4.9)

TABLE 4.10. *Number of TV Photo-Opportunities Party Leaders had during the Final Campaign*

	Thatcher	Kinnock	Steel and Owen	Steel	Owen
Item showing leaders as:					
Decisive	94	63	85	38	47
Caring	11	78	50	23	27
Willing to listen	34	38	59	26	33
Journalists contextualizing remarks suggesting leader is					
Tough/decisive/energetic/ well-informed	54	50	65	28	37
Caring/likeable/friendly/ willing to listen	28	44	41	15	26

how decisive or caring they were. Television journalists were very cautious. They seldom made negative remarks. What varied was the frequency of their positive remarks. Contextualizing remarks are potentially influential. Patterson (1980) found, in his study of an American presidential election, that public perceptions of who won televised presidential debates depended upon whether viewers had watched journalists analysing candidates' performances after the debates themselves.

Thatcher scored well on being tough and decisive. She displayed these qualities in photo-opportunities much more frequently than any other leader. But the journalists drew attention to her toughness only about as frequently as they drew attention to Kinnock's strong qualities. Conversely, in terms of photo-opportunities Kinnock did much better than any other leader on appearing 'caring', though not much better on appearing 'willing to listen'. Journalists' contextualizing remarks put him ahead on these softer virtues but only by a small margin. So the evidence suggests that journalists' contextualizing remarks tended to repeat the message of the photo-opportunities but much less clearly. Compared to photo-opportunities, journalists' remarks represented a shift towards a more equal balance between the parties.

Yet the most significant feature of journalists' remarks is the one which is easiest to overlook: their remarks, when they made them, were overwhelmingly positive. They enhanced the image of every leader in every party. They co-operated with all parties to present party leaders in a favourable light and were reluctant to balance praise with criticism in the tense atmosphere of an election campaign.

Party unity

We classified every headline and story in which a party appeared according to whether it implied that the party was united or disunited. Most television news items did neither, or hinted at elements of both. But very few (less than 5 per cent) of relevant items unambiguously implied disunity by showing spokesmen disagreeing amongst themselves, by interviewing party dissidents, or by referring to disagreements and tensions within a party. Over five times as many items (25 per cent) unambiguously implied party unity by showing a party's leaders endorsing each other and agreeing on policy, or by showing party leaders surrounded by enthusiastic party workers or appearing before an enthusiastic audience (Table 4.11)

TABLE 4.11. *Party Unity in the Final Campaign as reflected in TV News Items* (%)

	Conservative	Labour	Alliance
Unity	28	24	24
Disunity	3	7	4
Mixed/neutral/cold	70	69	72

During the pre-campaign week in March, we recorded *no* items which positively projected the unity of any party. These rather artificial news items were very much the product of the final campaign. During that final campaign, television projections of Conservative unity reached a peak in the third week; Labour got the most favourable coverage at the start and the end of the campaign; while the Alliance started well but finished badly (Table 4.12).

One of the main ways in which unity was projected (though not the only one) was by the video background to reports about party spokesmen. It is truly remarkable how few news items

TABLE 4.12. *Trends in Positive TV Projections of Party Unity* (%)

	Pre-campaign week	Final campaign				
		Week 1	Week 2	Week 3	Week 4	Week 5
Conservatives	0	25	32	33	27	20
Labour	0	27	25	22	20	27
Alliance	0	29	25	24	26	15
Con *minus* Lab	0	−2	7	11	7	−7

showed party spokesmen in company with their political opponents or even with ordinary members of the public. The most frequent location was no significant location at all: a 'talking head', a studio interview, an interview in a bus or plane, or even just a quote. After that, the most frequent locations were with supporters or with journalists.

In March, Thatcher's most frequent location was 'with Gorbachev' while Kinnock, Steel, and Owen appeared without locations as talking heads or quotes (Table 4.13). But the only international VIPs who appeared with party spokesmen during the final campaign were those assembled at the Venice summit. Reagan and Weinberger intervened briefly in the middle of the campaign as well and 'appeared' with party leaders in the same news items by means of video editing though not in person.

At the start of the final campaign, Labour and Conservative spokesmen appeared frequently with their own supporters but in the third week appearances with journalists suddenly became much more prominent. Obtrusive journalists pushing hard questions appeared in only 2 per cent of Labour spokesmen's contributions in the first week and only 5 per cent in the second, but 21 per cent in the third. The heat went off a bit after that but the early focus on party supporters never returned.

Steel and Owen appeared together in about half of their appearances during the first week of the campaign. One consequence was that these Alliance leaders were seldom shown with their own supporters during that week: 30 per cent of Labour and Conservative spokesmen's appearances were with their supporters, but only 5 per cent of Alliance spokesmen's. In a dramatic shift in tactics the Alliance leaders gave up their

'Tweedledum and Tweedledee' routine in the second week (though they appeared together quite frequently in the third, fourth and fifth weeks). There was then a correspondingly sharp rise in items showing Steel or Owen (*or* but not *and*!) with supporters and journalists. For the Alliance these two locations received roughly equal coverage with no such shift in the balance between supporters and journalists as occurred for Labour.

TABLE 4.13. *Trends in Spokesmen's Locations in TV News Items* (%)

	Pre-campaign week	Final campaign				
		Week 1	Week 2	Week 3	Week 4	Week 5
With VIPs						
Con spokesmen	41	0	0	2	0	13
Lab spokesmen	4	1	0	2	0	0
Lib spokesmen	0	0	0	0	0	0
SDP spokesmen	0	0	0	0	0	0
With supporters						
Con spokesmen	0	31	28	14	13	12
Lab spokesmen	6	28	30	11	9	13
Lib spokesmen	0	5	14	17	10	13
SDP spokesmen	0	5	13	16	13	13
With Steel/Owen						
Lib spokesmen with Owen	0	47	15	5	12	11
SDP spokesmen with Steel	0	50	16	5	9	5
With journalists						
Con spokesmen	0	5	8	16	15	15
Lab spokesmen	0	2	5	21	13	16
Lib spokesmen	0	2	17	15	19	11
SDP spokesmen	0	2	16	17	20	11

Party credibility

Television news items project party credibility in several ways. We noted whether television showed party rallies full with enthusiastic audiences or half-empty with unenthusiastic audiences; whether party leaders on walkabouts were greeted by ordinary people in a friendly fashion or whether they were shunned; whether party leaders were endorsed or criticized by

VIPs, especially foreign leaders; whether television reports of opinion polls indicated public support for the policies of the party; and whether television journalists' contextualizing comments implied public support or public rejection for each party. From all of these we formed a composite index of party credibility, as projected in television news bulletins.

In terms of this overall composite measure Labour received the most favourable coverage in television news (largely because it ran a more professional campaign with better photo-opportunities, etc.) and the Alliance the least favourable (Table 4.14). But all parties received strongly favourable coverage: news balance degenerated into non-comparative party advertising as television co-operated with the parties to screen their carefully staged non-events, their ticket-only rallies, and their atypical walkabouts.

Journalists' comments were markedly less favourable than other aspects of credibility projections, however. In terms of journalists' contextualizing the Conservatives scored better than Labour. Comments about the Alliance were almost as likely to be *un*favourable as favourable.

TABLE 4.14. *Projections of Party Credibility during the Final Campaign* (%)

	Con	Lab	All
Journalists' contextualizing comments	+42	+39	+9
Composite measure	+59	+65	+46

Notes: Entry is the percentage of positive credibility items *minus* the percentage of negative credibility items as a percentage of all relevant items.

Composite measure is based on rallies, walkabouts, VIPs, journalists' comments, and opinion polls.

In March, the Conservative Party enjoyed very high positive ratings both on our composite measure and in journalists' comments while Labour and the Alliance got substantial negative ratings (Table 4.15). News items projecting a positive rather than negative image of party credibility were 94 per cent more frequent for the Conservatives than for Labour. At the start of the final campaign every party received more favourable coverage than before, and the difference between the treatment of Labour and the Conservatives sank to only a quarter of what it had been in March. As the campaign progressed the Conservative advantage declined still more. It followed a 'rollercoaster' trend: a steep drop until the fourth week and then a partial recovery in the fifth.

TABLE 4.15. *Trends in Projections of Party Credibility* (%)

	Pre-campaign week	Final campaign				
		Week 1	Week 2	Week 3	Week 4	Week 5
Net positive contextualizing comments on:						
Conservatives	66	83	49	44	−14	68
Labour	−10	46	26	34	33	36
Alliance	−17	38	13	3	18	3
Con *minus* Lab	76	37	23	10	−47	32
Net positive overall projection of credibility for:						
Conservatives	71	91	62	64	24	73
Labour	−23	69	59	64	77	61
Alliance	−19	48	59	31	50	38
Con *minus* Lab	94	22	3	0	−53	12

On projections of party credibility Labour got as good treat-ment as the Conservatives in the second and third weeks of the campaign and very much better treatment than the Conservatives in the fourth, though the Conservatives regained a modest advantage in the fifth. So despite the defence controversy in the third week, Labour still managed to project a television image of a party that was popular in the country and gaining ground on the Conservatives. In the fourth week the debate shifted towards Labour's natural issue territory and a couple of polls (notably *Gallup* and BBC *Newsnight*) suggested the gap between Labour and the Conservatives was closing rapidly. Even in their own eyes, Conservative credibility (in the sense of looking like popular winners) declined sharply and led to the crisis of confidence in Conservative Central Office known as 'wobbly Thursday' (Tyler, 1987). Then, right at the end of the campaign, the Conservatives managed to project an image of confident success: new polls suggested that the *Gallup* and *Newsnight* polls were deviant rather than heralds of a trend, Thatcher went off to meet foreign VIPs at the Venice summit of Western nations, and Labour's Denis Healey was reduced to having an on-air row with a young *TV-am* presenter about his wife's use of private health care facilities.

CONCLUSIONS

This review of television news during the campaign has highlighted some significant patterns of television presentation:

1. Wherever there were explicit references to parties and leaders they tended to be unrealistically positive. During the final campaign parties were presented as united, leaders as both caring and decisive. Video images of party supporters, rallies, and VIPs helped to build up the image of all the parties while party dissidents seldom appeared.

2. The parties did *not* receive equal treatment—some got more coverage and more favourable treatment than others (though all of them were favourably treated). The Conservative government got two bites at the television cherry: once as a party, once as the government. Coverage in non-controversial news items was very heavily biased towards the Conservatives and especially so towards the end of the campaign. Controversial items tended to focus on the two-party Conservative versus Labour battle and again, this emphasis increased sharply towards the end of the campaign.

3. Television's issue agenda was very different from the public's agenda. People wanted parties to focus on social and economic issues, not security issues. But television coverage in explicitly election news was balanced between social and security issues, while television's background news items concentrated overwhelmingly on security issues. In the view of some political scientists this issue emphasis constitutes a right-wing bias.

5

Varieties of Television News

Different television news programmes operate under different constraints. This chapter compares the output of six television news programmes during the final campaign: the BBC's *Six O'Clock News, Nine O'Clock News,* and *Reporting Scotland;* and ITV's *News at 5.45, News at Ten,* and *Scotland Today.* These programmes appeared on two channels, BBC and ITV; they included early evening news and main evening news from the national newsrooms in London, and the main regional news programmes from Glasgow. If, as is sometimes claimed, 'the medium is the message', then we might expect to find clear differences between BBC and ITV, between the early and main evening news, between national and regional news, and between a very short programme like the fifteen-minute *News at 5.45* and the other longer news programmes—some of them specially extended to four times the length of *News at 5.45* during the election campaign.

To what extent did the programme dictate the message? Was the message influenced more by the news organization (BBC versus ITV) or by the inescapable technical features of the programme like its length and time of transmission, or by its news-brief, that is, its relationship to other news programmes?

PRESENTATION, CONTROVERSY, REVIEW, AND BACK-GROUND NEWS

Overall, about half the items on the national news were non-election, *background news* items. There was little consistent difference between channels or between the early and main news.

ITV's *News at 5.45* was unique in broadcasting no *review* items—clearly the result of its very short, fifteen-minute length which allowed no time for reflection, and relatively little for controversy.

There was no difference between the BBC and ITV in the balance between *presentation* and *controversy*, but early evening news contained much more party presentation and rather less controversy than the main news. Parties displayed their wares on the early news and debated with their opponents on the main news. This switch from party presentation in the early evening to controversy later in the evening was more pronounced on ITV, whose early and main news programmes differed more in length than the BBC's, and whose early news was earlier and main news later than the BBC's.

Scottish programmes screened less controversy *and* less party presentation than national programmes—much less election news of all kinds in fact. Two-thirds of Scottish news items were non-election, background news (Table 5.1).

TABLE 5.1. *Presentation, Controversy, Review, and Background News in the Campaign* (%)

	News programme					
	5.45	*Six*	*Nine*	*Ten*	*ST*	*RS*
Presentation	29	30	15	16	9	19
Controversy	14	21	23	26	16	16
Review	0	4	9	10	7	2
Background news	57	45	53	48	68	63

Note: Figures are percentages of all news items (headlines and stories) screened by the programme during the campaign. All tables in this chapter are based on the campaign itself and exclude the pre-campaign week.

The four basic categories of news were subdivided into twenty-six detailed subcategories. Amongst the subcategories of party presentation items we included *campaign trail* items in which television news followed a party's campaign but the coverage did not focus on a single issue. Campaign trail items comprised about 15 per cent of the early evening news but only 6 per cent of the main news and even less of the Scottish news. Conversely items in which one party *attacked* another party (or parties) were

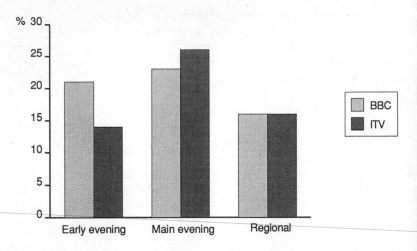

FIG. 5.1. Controversy on TV News by Programme (see Table 5.1)

twice as frequent on the main news as on the early news. (Party attacks were a subcategory of controversy items.)

Non-election news took a larger share of Scottish bulletins than of national, and a further subdivision of this type of item reveals an even more striking difference. Scottish bulletins were almost entirely *domestic* in their focus. So while about 24 per cent of the national bulletins (irrespective of channel or early/late timing) consisted of domestic non-election news, 61 per cent of Scottish bulletins did so. Conversely, while national bulletins devoted about 27 per cent of their items to *foreign* news, Scottish bulletins gave only 5 per cent to such news (Table 5.2).

This difference between Scottish and national television news is of immense importance. The difference does not exist on radio. BBC Radio Scotland news is an alternative to BBC Radio 4 national news, not a supplement. Consequently BBC Radio Scotland features national (that is, British) and international as well as Scottish news. It uses material from the BBC's London newsroom, telephone interviews linking Glasgow-based presenters with correspondents world-wide, and their own experts (from Scotland, England, and beyond) to comment on international affairs. It is broadcast simultaneously with BBC Radio 4 news and radio listeners cannot listen to both. But on television, the

TABLE 5.2. *Detailed Subcategories of News Items (%)*

	News programme					
	5.45	*Six*	*Nine*	*Ten*	*ST*	*RS*
Presentation included:						
Campaign trail	14	14	6	5	1	7
Govt in action	6	4	3	4	1	2
Controversy included:						
Attack	5	8	11	16	9	11
Damage limitation	2	4	4	2	4	2
Clash	4	5	6	4	2	2
Review:						
All categories of review	0	4	9	10	7	2
Non-election, background news included:						
Domestic British news	29	23	21	23	65	57
Foreign–British news	9	7	12	9	3	6
Purely foreign news	18	15	20	16	0	0

Note: Purely foreign news did not involve Britain; foreign–British news involved Britain and other countries.

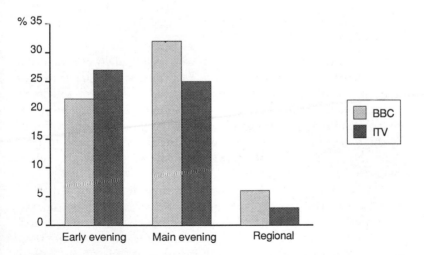

FIG. 5.2 Foreign Background News on TV by Programme (see Table 5.2.)

BBC's *Reporting Scotland* and Scottish Television's *Scotland Today* are almost entirely devoted to domestic and, indeed, Scottish news. They complement the BBC's *Six O'Clock News* and ITV's *News at 5.45* and are screened immediately after those national bulletins. Axford and Madgwick (1986) have noted that Scottish television news programmes 'bear comparison with national news in the range and complexity of their coverage'. Their 1986 content analysis showed that Scottish television news reports on employment and on nuclear fallout from Chernobyl, for example, gave more depth and detail than the national news. However, Scottish television news is similar to English regional television news in its overwhelming concentration on domestic affairs; in giving less coverage to 'government in action' and more coverage of local politicians—including locally based MPs; and in giving more equal coverage to all three parties (four in Scotland). So Scottish television news is really regional in a way that Scottish radio news is not. In that respect *Reporting Scotland* and *Scotland Today* represent other regional television news programmes tolerably well. (Hetherington, 1989a, describes Scottish coverage of the 1987 election campaign while Hetherington, 1989b, analyses regional news throughout Britain, from 'Plymouth Sound to Moray Firth'.)

THE ELECTION NEWS AGENDA: ISSUE COVERAGE IN ELECTION ITEMS

About a quarter of all election news items lacked a clear issue focus: 30 per cent of early evening news items, and 20 per cent of main evening news items. That reflected a tendency to screen unfocused campaign trail items in the early evening and more sharply defined, issue-based controversy later in the evening. Scottish regional news screened relatively few campaign trail items but 33 per cent of their election news still lacked a clear issue focus.

Campaign issues (including opinion polls and speculation about the parties' prospects) got a little more coverage on the main news than on the early news. The *Nine O'Clock News* and *News at Ten* were often able to reveal key points from the next day's newspaper polls. News interest in party prospects within Scotland was justified after the event when the Conservatives lost over half their Scottish seats while enjoying another land-slide victory in England. Appropriately, ITV's *Scotland Today* gave a lot of attention to the progress of the campaign in Scotland, though the BBC's *Reporting Scotland* did not.

Scottish news contained twice as much as national news on *party philosophy, economic, and social* issues but only half as much on *security* issues. The reasons are not hard to find. First, we included policy on self-government (Scottish devolution or in-dependence) as one aspect of party philosophy, and the entire difference in coverage of party philosophy is due to Scottish coverage of the devolution issue. Second, since Scottish television news (unlike Scottish radio news) was very much a regional supplement to national news, it seldom covered election debates about foreign policy and defence issues. That accounts for the entire shortfall of Scottish coverage of security issues. Scottish television still covered other security issues such as crime or law and order, but not military defence (Table 5.3).

TABLE 5.3. *The Election News Agenda: Coverage of Issues* (%)

	News programme					
	5.45	Six	Nine	Ten	ST	RS
Unfocused	29	31	22	17	30	36
Leadership	5	5	8	7	1	0
Philosophy	4	4	7	11	13	16
Economy	14	11	10	12	16	21
Physical security	21	20	18	21	7	12
Social security	8	12	9	10	8	10
Two nations	4	5	3	4	3	1
Special interests	1	2	3	2	2	0
Campaign progress	14	11	18	16	19	4

Note: Figures are percentages of election news items (i.e. of presentation, controversy, and review items).

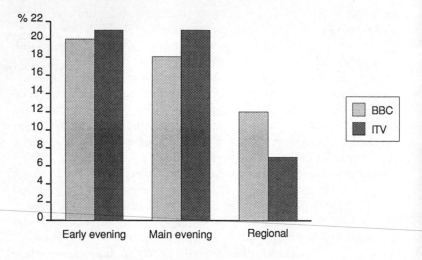

FIG. 5.3. Security Issues in Election News Items by Programme
(see Table 5.3.)

Retrospective and prospective orientations

By retrospective we mean a backward-looking evaluation of the
parties' records on the issues or, indeed, of the simple historical
record of past events. By prospective we mean a forward-looking
evaluation of party policy. We noted whether an issue was
treated as retrospective, prospective, or contemporaneous. For
example, the record of unemployment under the Thatcher government was *retrospective*; current levels of unemployment were
contemporaneous; and plans for employment training or policies
for reflation and job creation were *prospective*.

Usually retrospective evaluations focus on the government's
record but if parties have alternated in office then even opposition
parties may have a record to defend. Even as late as 1987, the
Conservatives campaigned on the 1978–9 'Winter of Discontent'
under the last Labour government. Prospective orientations
usually focus on the opposition's alternative policy for the future,
but a feature of the 1987 election was Prime Minister Thatcher's
personal commitment (only reluctantly abandoned in the heat of

the campaign) to fight on her government's new policies for the future—the 'next move forward'.

Roughly a quarter of election news items adopted a prospective orientation to the issues; most others adopted a contemporaneous orientation. There was no difference between national and regional news and little between BBC and ITV, but some evidence that a prospective, future-policy orientation was somewhat more frequent on the early evening news and a contemporaneous orientation somewhat more frequent on the main news (Table 5.4).

TABLE 5.4. *Retrospective and Prospective Issue Orientations* (%)

	News programme					
	5.45	Six	Nine	Ten	ST	RS
Retrospective	7	4	4	2	2	2
Contemporaneous	66	63	74	74	71	67
Prospective	27	33	22	23	27	31

Note: Figures are percentages of all election news items in which issues were mentioned.

The campaign period can be divided into five weeks (the last a mere three days prior to voting on Thursday 10 June, however). The election was declared at the start of week 1; party manifestos were issued at the start of week 2; Kinnock's unfortunate interview with David Frost on defence (speedily christened his 'dad's army' interview) came at the start of week 3. The election temperature cooled noticeably thereafter as attention switched back to domestic issues.

Generally, prospective orientations to issues peaked in week 2 and week 3 and dropped back sharply thereafter, that is, weeks 2 and 3 were 'policy weeks' while the other weeks were 'state of the nation weeks'. There were differences between news programmes, however. In the first week ITV concentrated on policy to a far greater extent than the BBC: 23 per cent of election news on ITV compared to 14 per cent on BBC. In a sense, ITV 'jumped the gun' on policy coverage. When the manifestos were issued in the second week early evening news and Scottish news gave between 35 and 44 per cent of their issue coverage to future policy. The main news gave only half as much. That reflected the fact that manifestos were launched at press conferences early in the day. In the third week, national news focused even more on future policy (between 39 and 55 per cent) while Scottish news eased back on policy items. During that third week national news covered the sharpening party controversy over defence while Scottish news, as purely regional programmes, did not (Table 5.5).

TABLE 5.5. *Trends in Prospective Issue Orientations* (%)

	News programme					
	5.45	*Six*	*Nine*	*Ten*	*ST*	*RS*
12–15 May Week 1	22	14	13	24	17	20
18–22 May Week 2	37	35	22	19	44	37
25–9 May Week 3	42	55	39	45	27	39
1–5 June Week 4	15	24	18	15	29	28
8–10 June Week 5	12	22	9	6	11	22

Note: Figures are the percentage of each week's election news items which adopted a prospective, rather than a retrospective or contemporaneous, orientation.

THE BACKGROUND NEWS AGENDA: ISSUE COVERAGE IN NON-ELECTION ITEMS

There is no sense in which most election news items could be described as 'good' or 'bad'; what might be good for one party would almost inevitably be bad for another. However, with most background news items it does make sense to ask whether the news was 'good' or 'bad', whether it seemed likely to encourage feelings of optimism or pessimism, happiness or despair. Our coders were instructed to code each item of non-election, background news as good or bad news about Britain's economy, crime prevention, defence, health, education, welfare, nationalization, privatization, foreign relations, or other (British) matters.

They also categorized foreign news as good or bad. We gave our coders specific examples of good and bad news of each kind, but relied heavily on their judgement.

There was almost no difference between BBC and ITV, nor between early and main national news in terms of net good news. However, foreign news was always much more unpleasant than British news. On average, good and bad news about Britain almost cancelled each other out, but bad foreign news was three times as frequent as good foreign news. As a result the national bulletins contained much more bad news than the Scottish regional bulletins. Even British news on the regional bulletins was more cheerful than on the national bulletins, however. So while national news programmes contained about 17 per cent more bad news than good, Scottish programmes contained about 5 per cent more good news than bad—a sharp contrast between news programmes that were screened in quick succession (Table 5.6)

TABLE 5.6. *Good and Bad Background News on TV* (%)

	News programme					
	5.45	Six	Nine	Ten	ST	RS
Good news about Britain	27	27	24	21	34	36
Bad news about Britain	27	31	26	24	29	32
Good foreign news	6	9	10	5	0	0
Bad foreign news	23	22	26	18	0	0
Net good news	−17	−17	−18	−16	5	4

Note: Figures are percentages of all background news items. Some background news was neither good nor bad.

Almost two-thirds of the background news items on the national bulletins and almost half on the regional bulletins dealt with subjects that were relevant to the issues under debate in the election campaign. Principally they dealt with security issues such as defence, crime, riots, and rebellion and to a much lesser extent with economic news. Differences between the BBC and ITV were negligible. There was a slight tendency for security issues to get greater coverage on main rather than early bulletins.

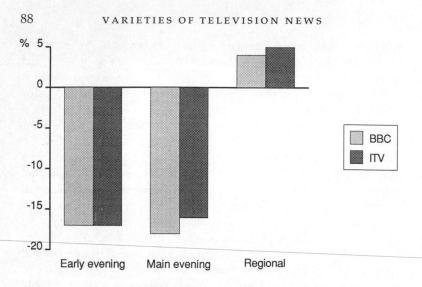

FIG. 5.4. Good News (Net) on TV by Programme (see Table 5.6)

But the principal contrast was between national and regional news: security issues got only half the coverage in background news on regional television that they received on national television because regional bulletins excluded foreign news which so often focused on security issues, although they included domestic law and order news. Conversely, news about the economy, the health service, and social welfare got twice as much coverage on regional bulletins as on national.

In addition, regional news contained significantly more non-political news: 55 per cent on regional bulletins compared to only 37 per cent on national bulletins. And its non-political news was different in kind as well as quantity. Non-political items on regional programmes included much more coverage of human interest stories, sport, and business news than national bulletins. Conversely, in marked contrast to national programmes, Scottish regional news provided almost no coverage of the Royal Family, nor of 'star' entertainers (Table 5.7).

HOW THE PARTIES WERE TREATED

Presentation items usually involved either just one of the major parties or all of them together. They seldom involved just two of

TABLE 5.7. *The Background News Agenda: Coverage of Issues* (%)

	News programme					
	5.45	*Six*	*Nine*	*Ten*	*ST*	*RS*
Economy	8	9	8	9	12	14
Security	46	44	53	48	24	21
Social	3	1	1	0	5	7
Non-political	37	38	33	39	55	55

Note: Figures are percentages of all background news items.

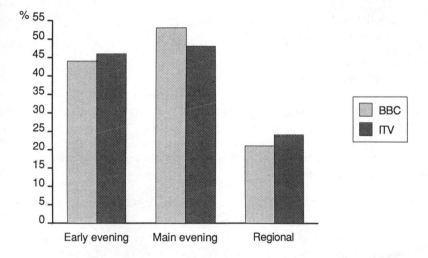

FIG. 5.5. Security Issues in TV Background News Items by Programme
(see Table 5.7)

the three main parties on the national news or just two or three of the four main Scottish parties on the Scottish news.

As we saw in the previous chapter, the Conservatives received a large amount of coverage in their role as government ministers as well as in their role as party politicians. There were markedly less such government in action items on the Scottish regional news but, taking their dual party/government roles together, the Conservatives got well over twice as much coverage in presentation items as either Labour or the Alliance on every news programme, including Scottish news.

Naturally, a distinguishing feature of Scottish regional news programmes was the attention they gave to the Scottish National Party (SNP). In presentation items the SNP got slightly more coverage than Labour or the Alliance but a lot less than the Conservatives (Table 5.8).

TABLE 5.8. *How the Parties were Covered in Presentation Items* (%)

	News programme					
	5.45	Six	Nine	Ten	ST	RS
Govt in action	24	13	21	24	6	12
Conservatives (as a party)	23	23	23	23	25	29
Labour	16	18	17	12	8	12
Alliance	18	18	13	23	11	9
Nationalists	4	2	0	3	23	17

Notes: Figures are percentages of all 'party presentation' items screened on each programme.

The Nationalist percentage includes any items where the Scottish SNP or the Welsh Plaid Cymru were prominent irrespective of what other parties also appeared.

The most frequent form of *controversy* involved a two-party battle between Labour and the Conservatives. Patterns of controversy were remarkably similar, in many aspects, across all the programmes. On Scottish news about 20 per cent of controversy items involved the SNP in conflict with Labour or, more often, the Conservatives. But while Scottish news had to take account of the different political situation north of the border, that did not prevent a very considerable focus on the Labour–Conservative battle: 35 per cent on *Scotland Today* and 21 per cent on *Reporting Scotland*, compared to an average of 38 per cent on the national news (Table 5.9).

Quite separately from our classification of news items into presentation or controversy items, we assessed the treatment of the parties by coding, for each appearance of each party, whether it was allowed to *present* itself (its policy, its leaders, or whatever)

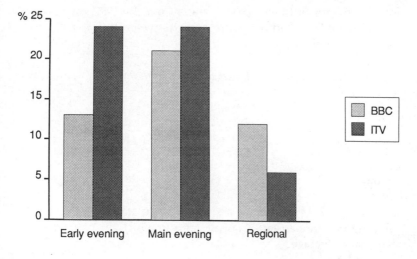

FIG. 5.6. Government in Action on TV by Programme (see Table 5.8)

TABLE 5.9. *How the Parties were Covered in Controversy Items* (%)

	News programme					
	5.45	*Six*	*Nine*	*Ten*	*ST*	*RS*
Con and Lab	37	33	36	41	35	21
Con and Alln	10	9	11	8	8	10
Lab and Alln	8	9	7	9	0	5
All main parties together	14	23	25	23	20	13
Nat and Con	0	0	0	0	10	25
Nat and Lab	0	0	0	0	5	0
Nat and Alln	0	0	0	0	0	2

Note: Figures are percentages of all 'controversy' items screened on each programme.

without any balancing or contradicting statements; or whether its presentation was *balanced,* or *contradicted,* or even *attacked* by other parties or journalists. Uncritical presentation of a party was more frequent on the early evening news and less frequent on the main evening news. There was a small but consistent tendency for ITV to present less critical items than the BBC on national news but in Scotland this difference between BBC and ITV was decisively reversed (Table 5.10).

TABLE 5.10. *Presentation without Balance, Contradiction, or Attack* (%)

	News programme					
	5.45	Six	Nine	Ten	ST	RS
Conservatives	40	39	30	39	50	83
Labour	42	35	27	28	45	69
Alliance	52	52	43	52	47	91

Note: Figures are percentages of all items in which the party received significant coverage.

Party leaders

Party leaders quite consciously try (especially in election campaigns) to convey messages just by appearing in particular places or with particular people.

National news 'located' party spokesmen in 60 per cent of relevant items, though ITV made more use of locations than the BBC. But Scottish regional news hardly ever placed party spokesmen in a visual context—preferring instead to use mainly 'talking heads' supplemented by a few 'quotes'. It was not that Scottish bulletins failed to use film to get away from the studio; they did, especially for a series of constituency reports, but not as video backgrounds for party spokesmen. Locational backgrounds were used in only 6 per cent of relevant Scottish news items but in 54 per cent of BBC national news items and 65 per cent of ITV national news items.

There was also a striking difference between the early and main evening news: on the main news (as contrasted with the early news), spokesmen were more than twice as likely to be shown against a background of supporters and less than half as likely to be shown with a crowd of journalists. This difference reflects the rhythm of a conventional campaign: press conferences in the morning, chats to journalists in the afternoon, and a rally with supporters in the evening: a tried and tested formula. (Table 5.11).

Searching for objective indicators of subjective images, we specified lists of actions and events that we felt implied that a party leader was 'decisive', or 'caring', or 'willing to listen'. In addition, our coders noted any contextualizing' comments by

TABLE 5.11. *Spokesmen's Locations in TV News Items (%)*

	News programme					
	5.45	*Six*	*Nine*	*Ten*	*ST*	*RS*
Conservative spokesmen (usually Thatcher)						
With supporters	9	12	22	31	5	9
With journalists	27	20	13	11	0	0
No location	38	49	46	31	90	86
Labour spokesmen (usually Kinnock)						
With supporters	13	9	21	28	7	0
With journalists	16	15	10	7	2	0
No location	39	50	51	41	90	100
Liberal spokesmen (usually Steel)						
With Owen	23	17	21	15	0	0
With ordinary people	13	12	6	9	0	0
With supporters	8	4	13	23	3	0
With journalists	18	20	7	5	3	0
No location	25	35	48	38	93	93
SDP spokesmen (usually Owen)						
With Steel	18	16	18	14	0	0
With ordinary people	10	11	5	9	0	0
With supporters	6	5	17	21	4	0
With journalists	18	20	9	6	4	0
No location	28	37	46	37	93	100

Note: Figures are percentages of items in which a party spokesman appeared. (Figures for *Reporting Scotland* are based on first three weeks of campaign only.)

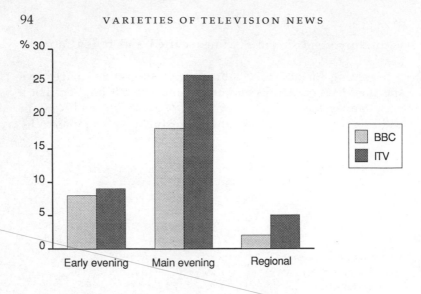

FIG. 5.7. Spokesmen with Supporters on TV News by Programme
(see Table 5.11)

television presenters which implied a party leader was 'tough or weak', 'tender or cold-hearted'. The sheer quantity of image-relevant items and contextualizing remarks varied between programmes. ITV's *News at 5.45* had exactly half as much as the average main evening news or BBC's early evening news, and Scottish news had almost none. Clearly there was no real difference between the BBC and ITV, as comparison of their main evening bulletins shows, but there was less time available for superfluous contextualizing comment on the very short *News at 5.45*, and very little coverage of national party leaders on regional news.

Party unity

The course of British politics over the last decade is frequently described in terms of Labour's disunity. A split amongst the Labour leadership led to the formation of the SDP in 1981 and the subsequent formation of the Liberal–SDP Alliance. Labour's 1983 general election campaign collapsed a fortnight before election day as its most senior remaining leaders quarrelled over defence policy. Many of the old suspicions about Labour disunity were resurrected in the Greenwich by-election shortly before the 1987 campaign.

On the other side, it is remarkable how few of Mrs Thatcher's original cabinet remained with her in 1987. As for the Alliance, which claimed to be a model for how different parties could work together in coalition without losing their separate identities, it collapsed in acrimonious discord within a week of the 1987 election result; evidence of that possibility was available long before the election, though it received less attention during the final campaign. Similarly, those who follow the progress of Scottish politics would have no difficulty pointing to evidence of personality and policy conflicts within the SNP. In short, Labour had no monopoly of disunity.

There was a sharp contrast between news coverage of parties outside the campaign period, which tended to stress disunity, and coverage within the campaign which grossly overemphasized the monolithic unity of every party. The election was presented as a battle between Conservative, Labour, and the Alliance nationally, with the addition of the SNP in Scotland. It was not presented as a battle by Thatcher to maintain her crumbling position within the Conservative Party (restored only by her unexpectedly large electoral victory, and only temporarily even then); nor as a battle by Kinnock to establish complete mastery over his polyarchic Labour movement; nor as a personal and political contest between Steel and Owen. Yet these were all important aspects of the 1987 election campaign.

We asked our coders to assess the extent to which every news item about a party contributed towards an image of unity or disunity. *Disunity* was implied by party spokesmen criticizing each other or disagreeing on policy; by party dissidents stating a viewpoint contrary to the party line; or by journalists referring to disagreements and tensions within the party. *Unity* was implied by party leaders endorsing each other as people or reinforcing each others' statements on policy; or by positive evidence of unity at a non-élite level—a video clip of a leader surrounded by enthusiastic supporters or addressing an enthusiastic audience at a rally.

Very few items on Scottish regional news seemed at all relevant to the concept of party unity, and most of the handful that were relevant implied disunity. National news was entirely different.

It included many news items indicating unity, disunity, or a mixture of both. While the majority of relevant items on national news programmes presented a mixed image, 25 per cent presented an unambiguously positive image of unity and only 5 per cent showed unambiguous evidence of disunity. Overwhelmingly, therefore, national (but not regional) television news reinforced party images of unity.

The sheer quantity of items emphasizing unity (of all parties) was greater on the main evening news than on early news, and greater on ITV than on BBC. ITV's *News at Ten*, in particular, put twice as much emphasis on party unity as the other three national bulletins. Analysis of the subcategories of our unity codes helps to explain this finding. Comparing ITV's *News at Ten* with the BBC's *Nine O'Clock News* shows that they gave approximately the same amount of coverage to items in which party leaders emphasized unity by supporting each other's policy statements and/or endorsing each other as personalities. But ITV's *News at Ten* gave much more coverage to party rallies, showing enthusiastic audiences and/or party leaders surrounded by enthusiastic party supporters. Since rallies generally took place in the evening, this difference probably reflected the extra hour available to the ITV team for gathering and processing their video material (Table 5.12).

TABLE 5.12. *Portrayal of Party Unity by TV News (%)*

		News programme			
		5.45	Six	Nine	Ten
Conservatives:	Disunity	2	1	2	5
	Unity	18	20	28	45
Labour:	Disunity	7	4	10	8
	Unity	21	16	20	38
Alliance:	Disunity	8	4	1	1
	Unity	23	18	21	34

Note: Figures are percentages of all items that implied unity, disunity, or a mixture of the two. An item showing a party rally but a mainly silent audience would count as 'mixed', for example. Scottish regional programmes screened so few items that met our criteria for implying party unity or disunity that they have been excluded from the table.

Party credibility

By 'credibility' we mean an image that suggests a party is competent to win office and competent to hold office—that it is a serious contender.

We used six different measures of credibility images in television news items and a composite credibility index. The main advantage of the composite index is that it was based upon many more news items than any one of the individual credibility indicators, that is, it combined the images conveyed by party rallies, leaders' tours, endorsement by VIPs, and favourable comments by journalists.

On credibility as on the more specific question of unity, television news generally collaborated with all the parties and screened items which built up their credibility. Overall our composite credibility index shows a *net* positive score of 65 per cent for Labour, 59 per cent for the Conservatives, and 46 per cent for the Alliance on the national news.

On ITV the parties' net composite credibility index was 70 per cent for Labour, 68 per cent for the Conservatives, and 64 per cent for the Alliance—very similar ratings for each of the three parties. On the BBC, however, party credibility scores were lower and more discriminating: 62 per cent for Labour and 51 per cent for the Conservatives but only 28 per cent for the Alliance.

Labour scored particularly well on the early evening news, and the Alliance particularly badly on the main evening news. That reflected the different content of early and main news. Early evening news reported the leaders' tours and visits. Kinnock's well-planned and well-executed touring schedule produced almost uniformly favourable coverage on all programmes, in sharp contrast to Thatcher's. Thatcher was burdened by a tooth abscess which affected her personal style, and by the need for elaborate security protection. She had nearly fallen victim to an IRA terrorist bomb in 1984. Overall, the net positive rating for Kinnock's tours on national news was 95 per cent compared to only 68 per cent for Thatcher. Later in the evening, the main news contained more coverage of rallies, on which the Alliance scored particularly badly, and much greater attempts at placing the election news in context, on which the Alliance scored even worse.

Journalists' contextualizing comments on national news were, on balance, 42 per cent favourable about the Conservatives, 39 per cent favourable about Labour, but only a mere 9 per cent favourable about the Alliance. Indeed, while ITV journalists' remarks about the Alliance were moderately favourable, BBC journalists' comments on *News at Six* were balanced, and on *News at Nine* they were moderately negative.

ITV journalists generally made much more favourable comments than BBC journalists about all the parties: 36 per cent more favourable about the Alliance, 12 per cent more favourable about Labour, and 17 per cent more favourable about the Conservatives. Given the very favourable light in which all the parties were presented on all the national news programmes, it is difficult to avoid the conclusion that ITV was afflicted by an excessive desire to speak well about everyone and everything.

Scottish regional news had to report an entirely different political situation. It would have been absurd for it to have implied the same pattern of party credibility as in the UK as a whole. After all, the Conservatives were heading for a record defeat in Scotland. On Scottish regional news, our composite credibility index gave Labour a net positive score of 52 per cent while the Conservatives scored only 11 per cent and the Alliance 15 per cent. In Scotland, the BBC was more favourable to every party than ITV, reversing the national pattern.

Scottish journalists seemed generally less afflicted with an excess of good feeling: for example, even their comments about Labour's credibility in Scotland were less favourable than their London colleagues' comments about Labour's credibility nationally, despite Labour's much greater electoral support north of the border (Table 5.13).

CONCLUSIONS: THE PROGRAMME AND THE MESSAGE

Television news on different programmes was different. Clearly the programme did determine the message. But how much? And what were the key characteristics that affected the message: rival news organizations, technical factors, or news-briefs?

TABLE 5.13. *Net Positive Credibility as reflected by TV News (%)*

	News programme					
	5.45	*Six*	*Nine*	*Ten*	*ST*	*RS*
Conservatives						
Journalists' contextualization	43	43	24	59	−27	−11
Composite index	64	61	41	72	0	22
Labour						
Journalists' contextualization	80	50	16	9	21	25
Composite index	91	76	47	48	40	64
Alliance						
Journalists' contextualization	36	8	−25	18	−30	0
Composite index	76	43	12	52	4	25

Note: These are *net* figures, calculated by subtracting the percentage of negative items from the percentage of positive items.

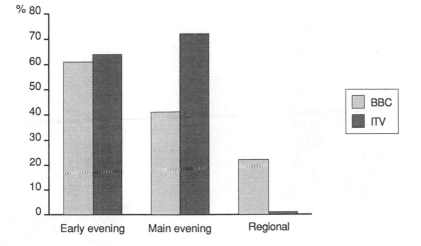

FIG. 5.8. Conservative Credibility as reflected in TV News by Programme (see Table 5.13)

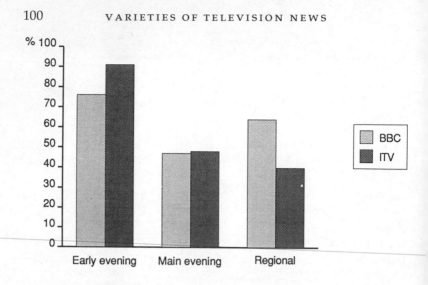

FIG. 5.9. Labour Credibility as reflected in TV News by Programme
(see Table 5.13)

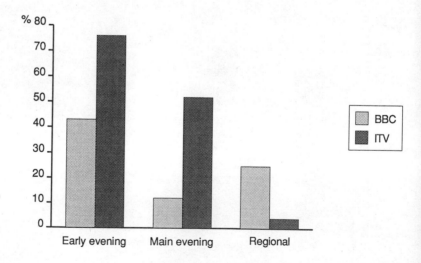

FIG. 5.10. Alliance Credibility as reflected in TV News by Programme
(see Table 5.13)

BBC versus ITV

When politicians complain about differences in news presentation they imply that a news organization is at fault. The striking feature of our findings is that the similarities between BBC and ITV news greatly exceeded the differences. None the less there was some consistency to the BBC–ITV differences: ITV was less critical of the parties, it emphasized party unity even more than the BBC, it gave the parties higher credibility scores, and it differentiated less between the credibility of different parties. In sum, ITV's treatment of the parties was more bland and supportive than the BBC's, though the party coverage on both networks was biased towards all of the parties, verging away from balanced news reporting and towards advertising.

ITV also moved heavily into policy analysis a week earlier than the BBC and screened less of the Steel–Owen double act at the start of the campaign. ITV made more use of video backgrounds to locate party leaders—which partly explains how it presented parties in a more favourable light, since video backgrounds were usually supportive.

Technical Factors

Next we come to the difference between the early and main evening news, and the special consequences of ITV's *News at 5.45* being so short and ITV's *News at Ten* enjoying an extra hour of preparation time. These technical factors were more influential determinants of news content than the organizational difference between the BBC and ITV.

For purely technical reasons, early evening bulletins reflected news events from the earlier part of the day while the main bulletins reflected the events of the evening. This simple technicality had a whole string of consequences:

1. Early evening news showed the leaders with journalists or on walkabouts rather than at rallies; so the early news favoured Labour since Kinnock's tours were so well planned, so well executed, and so little hampered by security restrictions.

2. The main evening news showed rallies which emphasized (indeed overemphasized) the unity of all the parties.

3. The early evening news was less sharply focused on specific issues because photo-opportunities are a lot less focused than clips from speeches.

4. The main evening news, consisting of long, specially extended programmes coming near the end of the day, was more reflective and had more review items; it was less prospective in its treatment of issues, more oriented towards a 'state of the nation' approach; its journalists offered more contextualizing comments; and it screened more opinion polls on the progress of the campaign.

5. ITV in particular changed its style sharply between its very short early news and its much longer main news. *News at 5.45* was so short that it included no review items, few controversies to which all three parties contributed, and only half as many leader-image items as any other news programme. Conversely, *News at Ten* was so late that it could give greater coverage to party rallies and so it emphasized party unity twice as much as other programmes.

News-briefs

Different news-briefs for national and regional news programmes also produced a string of consequences:

1. Because foreign news was excluded from the range of topics allowed on regional news, their news agenda included a lot less about security issues and a lot more about economic and social issues or party philosophy. In the view of most political scientists that meant regional news was inevitably more left-wing than national news. Because this is an automatic consequence of a technicality, it probably applied to all regional news programmes, not just to Scottish ones.

2. Because foreign news was generally bad news, regional bulletins contained a lot less bad news: they were distinctly cheerful compared to national news. Even their domestic news was more cheerful as well as being less metropolitan, however.

3. By definition, national party leaders can tour any one region relatively infrequently. So regional news seldom covered British party leaders. It gave more weight to locally based politicians.

4. In turn, that meant regional news had less motivation to screen 'campaign trail' items following party spokesmen round

photo-opportunity locations. So regional television separated party argument, which it screened without backgrounds, from photo-journalism, which in Scotland focused on places (constituency reports) rather than people (leaders) as on the national news.

5. One consequence of not following leaders round photo-opportunities and party rallies was that regional news did much less to build images of party unity and party enthusiasm compared to national news.

6. Regional journalists were also much less likely to add supportive contextualizing remarks than national journalists, though regional news editors were more inclined to screen items that allowed a party to present its case without being balanced by attacks from other parties.

7. And, of course, regional news bulletins in Scotland covered devolution, the SNP, and the state of party support in Scotland much more extensively than national news. They could hardly avoid that.

Within Scotland, there were differences between the BBC and ITV. Interestingly they were almost the inverse of the national differences. In its national news programmes, ITV was more bland, more supportive of all the parties; but in regional news programmes, the BBC's *Reporting Scotland* screened more trail items than *Scotland Today*, the BBC was more generous to the credibility of all the parties and quite unique in the way it presented party viewpoints without contradiction from other parties. Clearly there was no such thing as a BBC style that applied to BBC programmes throughout the network.

Our analysis of regional news has focused on one of the most distinctive regions, where separate institutions like the Scottish National Party, the Scottish Office, and the Secretary of State for Scotland raised the significance of unique regional issues. But some of the most important features of Scottish regional television applied to regional television throughout Britain, above all the fact that it was limited to providing a regional supplement to national news and could therefore give very little coverage to foreign and defence issues or to national (British) party leaders.

Could television news be different?

Have we reached the comforting conclusion that BBC and ITV news programmes were unbiased? That the differences between the BBC and ITV were small and inconsistent (the opposite in Glasgow from London, for example)? That purely technical factors shaped television's presentation of the news? Despite the significance of technical factors, the answer must be: 'No'.

Competitive pressures may reduce product differentiation, so that programmes become similar to the particular programmes that they regard as direct competitors. It is a familiar theory in economics that while two major producers who dominate a market may converge to reduce uncertainty, they need not converge on the product that the public wants. As long as they converge (on anything) they can enjoy a safe, if not exciting, existence.

Thus the two early national news programmes may be driven towards similarity by competition as well as by the reality of the world they report; just as competition may influence the two main national news programmes and the two Scottish regional programmes towards similarity. No doubt journalists on these programmes are most keenly aware of the differences between their own programme and its principal competitor, but from the outside, the similarities are more striking than the differences.

Yet we have no evidence that these similarities are the inevitable result of a faithful reflection of some objective reality rather than the result of competitive pressures to avoid being different. None of the television news agendas came anywhere near the stated wishes of the electorate, though regional news came closer than national. Perhaps the electorate were wrong. Perhaps the television news agenda *should not* have been different. But clearly it *could* have been very different, simply by coming closer to the electorate's stated priorities.

In many other ways, too, television news programmes could have been different but consciously or unconsciously chose one particular formula. Regional news programmes managed to report the election, with plenty of location pictures, but without trailing round after the party leaders from photo-opportunity to ticket-only rally. The national news could have done the same but chose not to. The emphasis, particularly by national news programmes, on party unity during the campaign contrasts sharply with their own focus on internal party disagreements at other times. That, too, could have been different. The networks' decision to give the parties equal coverage could have been different; so could their apparent decision to omit 'government in action' items from calculations about equal party coverage; so could their focus upon the Conservative–Labour battle in controversy items. This list of ways in which the news programmes could have been different could be extended. We have shown a degree of convergence between pairs of programmes that were in competition for the same audience. We have not shown that this convergence reflected objective news realities, nor viewers' wishes.

6

Public Reactions to the Media

Media analysts have generally concluded that British newspapers were highly partisan while British broadcasting was not. We have argued that even broadcasting was biased towards the right wing and, separately, towards the government of the day. But how did the public react? If the bias we have detected in broadcasting was not obvious to media specialists we can hardly expect that it would have been obvious to the general public. Even the much greater bias in the press may have seemed less obvious to them. After all, they choose to buy their own newspapers and may be bound, psychologically, to defend their own chosen paper even if they accept that other people's papers are biased.

PUBLIC PERCEPTIONS OF MEDIA BIAS

In fact, our panel survey shows that public perceptions of media bias mirror expert opinion remarkably closely. About a quarter thought the BBC was biased in its treatment of the Conservative government; rather less felt it was biased in its treatment of other parties. Only one elector in seven thought ITV was biased in its treatment of the Conservatives and, again, rather less felt it was biased in its treatment of other parties. In terms of the *total* percentage who alleged bias on television, those who actually watched BBC or ITV news were slightly more inclined to allege bias (Table 6.1). (For corroborative figures see McGregor, Svennevig, and Ledger, 1989; Gunter, Svennevig, and Wober, 1986, p. 82.)

Many of these perceptions of bias cancelled out however. Some people alleged a bias *towards* the Conservatives, while others alleged a bias *against* the Conservatives, for example. On balance, the public felt that bias on both channels favoured the Conservative Party and the Conservative Party alone. Perceptions of net bias on ITV were very small indeed, the numbers who

detected an anti-Conservative bias almost (but not quite) equal-
ling those who saw a pro-Conservative bias. Opinion was also
divided about BBC bias but rather more people detected a pro-
Conservative, anti-Labour bias on the BBC than on ITV. Both
BBC viewers and those who did not watch the BBC were agreed
on balance that it was biased towards the Conservatives though
those who actually watched it were more evenly divided on the
direction of BBC bias than those who did not (Table 6.1 again).
(For corroborative figures see IBA, 1987, p. 17.)

TABLE 6.1. *Public Perceptions of Bias on BBC and ITV News* (%)

	Bias towards party (a)	Bias against party (b)	Neither (c)	DK (d)	Total bias (a+b)	Net bias (a−b)
BBC-TV news						
Amongst BBC-TV news viewers						
— about Conservatives	15	9	75	1	24	6
— about Labour	8	12	79	1	20	−4
— about Alliance	3	7	88	2	10	−4
Amongst those who did not watch BBC-TV news						
— about Conservatives	18	5	51	26	23	13
— about Labour	4	10	59	27	14	−6
— about Alliance	3	5	64	28	8	−2
ITV news						
Amongst ITV news viewers						
— about Conservatives	9	6	82	4	15	3
— about Labour	6	6	85	4	12	0
— about Alliance	3	4	88	5	7	−1
Amongst those who did not watch ITV news						
— about Conservatives	7	4	53	36	11	3
— about Labour	5	5	55	36	10	0
— about Alliance	2	3	58	37	5	−1

Notes: Entries are averages of figures for First Fortnight and Second
Fortnight Campaign Waves.
   BBC and ITV viewers defined as those who had watched the relevant
news on the day of the interview or the day before.

In sharp contrast, three quarters of all newspaper readers said that the papers they had read on the day of the interview were biased in their coverage of the Conservative and Labour Parties, though less than half said their papers gave biased coverage of the Alliance. (For earlier findings on public perceptions of press bias see Kellner and Worcester, 1982; Butler and Stokes, 1969.)

The direction of bias varied from paper to paper. Roughly four-fifths of *Sun*, *Express*, *Mail*, and *Telegraph* readers said their paper was biased towards the Conservatives, while a similar number of *Mirror* readers said their paper was biased against the Conservatives. Somewhat fewer readers of the *Star* and the *Guardian* saw a Conservative versus Labour bias in their papers though, on balance, they thought the *Star* was pro-Conservative and the *Guardian* anti-Conservative. A substantial minority of all paper readers, 42 per cent, thought their paper was biased in its treatment of the Alliance; and most of those who did detect bias thought their paper was biased against the Alliance. *Guardian* readers were exceptional, however. Over half the *Guardian*'s readers thought the paper was biased towards the Alliance, while a mere 5 per cent thought it was biased against (Table 6.2).

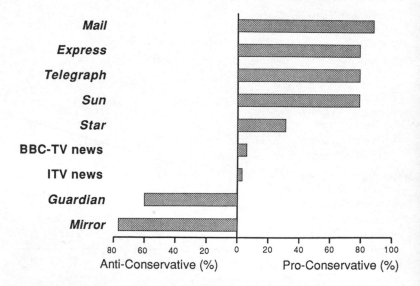

FIG. 6.1. Perceptions of Net Bias towards the Conservatives
(see Tables 6.1 and 6.2)

TABLE 6.2. *Public Perceptions of Press Bias* (%)

	Bias towards party (a)	Bias against party (b)	Total bias (a+b)	Net bias (a−b)
About Conservatives amongst readers of				
Sun	80	1	81	79
Star	42	11	53	31
Express	81	2	83	79
Mail	89	1	90	88
Mirror	4	81	85	−77
Telegraph	79	0	79	79
Guardian	0	60	60	−60
All paper readers	49	27	76	22
About Labour amongst readers of				
Sun	4	81	85	−77
Star	18	37	55	−19
Express	2	78	80	−76
Mail	1	74	75	−73
Mirror	88	2	90	86
Telegraph	0	70	70	−70
Guardian	39	8	47	31
All paper readers	28	44	72	−16
About Alliance amongst readers of				
Sun	3	46	49	−43
Star	6	26	32	−20
Express	2	45	47	−43
Mail	2	36	38	−34
Mirror	4	45	49	−41
Telegraph	3	34	37	−31
Guardian	53	5	58	48
All paper readers	7	35	42	−28

Notes: Entries are averages of figures for First Fortnight and Second Fortnight Waves.

Based on those who had read the named paper on the day of the interview. Very few readers replied 'don't know' about their own paper; so, apart from the tabulated percentages who alleged different kinds of bias, nearly all the rest denied their paper was biased.

WHO ALLEGED MEDIA BIAS?

Overall, readers of highbrow papers were less likely to allege bias in their own paper than readers of middlebrow or lowbrow papers but the differences were surprisingly small. In the first fortnight of the campaign readers of highbrow and lowbrow papers detected the same amount of bias in coverage of the Conservatives and the Alliance, though highbrow readers found less bias in coverage of Labour. As the campaign drew to a close, however, readers of lowbrow papers detected significantly more bias.

Readers of right-wing papers were well aware of their papers' pro-Conservative and anti-Labour bias though less unanimous about their papers' anti-Alliance bias. Conversely those who read left-wing papers were largely agreed that they were anti-Conservative and pro-Labour but more divided on whether they had an anti-Alliance bias. Perceptions of both total and net bias increased during the campaign. Readers of right-wing papers became more aware of their pro-Conservative, anti-Labour bias while readers of left-wing papers became more aware of their anti-Conservative, pro-Labour bias (Table 6.3).

Age, education, ideology, even strength of partisanship, had little influence over whether or not people perceived bias on television or in their papers. Detection of bias was also unrelated to motivations for following the campaign or interest in politics during the campaign. However, those who had expressed a general interest in politics during the parliamentary mid-term were more likely to see bias on the television and in their papers early in the campaign. Towards the end of the campaign perceptions of bias became more widespread (Table 6.4).

Partisanship and allegations of bias

The direction of alleged bias was related in a complex way to the critics' own partisanship. People tended to see television as biased against their own party while they thought their paper was biased towards their own party. They asserted, rather than denied, the bias in their own preferred papers. No doubt they chose their paper partly with that bias in mind.

The correlation between being Conservative and alleging *anti-*

TABLE 6.3. *Trends in Perceived Bias by Types of Paper* (%)

	Total bias		Net bias	
	FF	SF	FF	SF
About Conservatives amongst readers of				
Lowbrow paper	69	80	69	70
Middlebrow paper	83	88	9	−7
Highbrow paper	68	69	29	32
Right-wing paper	77	84	76	79
Left-wing paper	78	82	−67	−81
About Labour amongst readers of				
Lowbrow paper	76	81	−61	−69
Middlebrow paper	80	87	3	14
Highbrow paper	55	55	−29	−35
Right-wing paper	71	78	−65	−73
Left-wing paper	81	85	72	82
About Alliance amongst readers of				
Lowbrow paper	42	47	−37	−39
Middlebrow paper	39	52	−35	45
Highbrow paper	42	38	0	−2
Right-wing paper	41	42	−33	−37
Left-wing paper	40	60	−19	−34

Note: Net perceptions of bias defined as for Table 6.1.

Conservative bias on the BBC rose from 24 per cent in the first fortnight of the campaign to 32 per cent in the second. There were almost identical correlations (and trends in correlations) between being Labour and alleging anti-Labour bias on the BBC. And the same general pattern applied, in a much weaker form, to allegations about ITV. By contrast, the correlation between being Conservative and alleging *pro*-Conservative bias in the respondent's own paper rose from 28 per cent in the first fortnight of the campaign to 39 per cent in the second.

TABLE 6.4. *Correlations between Generalized Interest in Politics and Perceptions of Bias*

Perception of bias	On BBC		On ITV		In paper	
	FF	SF	FF	SF	FF	SF
About Conservatives	23	14	11	8	14	6
About Labour	16	13	13	7	9	2
About Alliance	15	13	5	6	11	16

Note: Generalized interest measured in the Mid-Term Wave (1986).

The correlation between allegations of bias and newspapers' actual partisanship (as defined in the footnote to Table 6.5) was twice as strong, however. Perceptions of newspaper bias depended more on the partisanship of the paper being read than on the partisanship of the reader who read it. (Table 6.5).

By a majority of 51 per cent at the start of the campaign, rising to 58 per cent at the end, Conservative partisans claimed that their paper was biased towards the Conservative Party. A smaller majority of Labour partisans asserted that their papers had a pro-Labour bias (22 per cent rising to 32 per cent). Alliance partisans admitted that they read anti-Alliance papers but they claimed their papers were less pro-Conservative than Conservative partisans' papers and less pro-Labour than Labour partisans' papers (Table 6.6).

In complete contrast Conservative and Labour partisans claimed that television news, particularly BBC news, was biased against their party. By the end of the campaign a majority of 12 per cent amongst Conservatives claimed the BBC was anti-Conservative and even more claimed it was pro-Labour. At the same time a majority of 23 per cent of Labour partisans claimed the BBC was pro-Conservative and anti-Labour. Labour partisans also claimed the BBC was anti-Alliance (Table 6.7).

We have to be careful to compare like with like when comparing different elements of the media. Conservative and Labour partisans who disagreed so strongly about bias on the BBC were all viewing the same source. But Conservative and Labour partisans who disagreed about the bias in their daily papers were reading different papers.

TABLE 6.5. *Correlations between Allegations of Bias and Partisanship of Electors and Papers*

	About Con		About Lab		About Alln	
	FF	SF	FF	SF	FF	SF
Electors' own partisanship	Correlation with perception of net bias on BBC					
Conservative	−24	−32	24	31	16	10
Labour	22	27	−23	−31	−11	−14
Alliance	3	9	−3	−3	−6	−3
Electors' own partisanship	Correlation with perception of net bias on ITV					
Conservative	−9	−12	7	9	3	6
Labour	5	15	−6	−7	1	−11
Alliance	6	−3	−2	−3	−5	4
Electors' own partisanship	Correlation with perceptions of net bias in paper read					
Conservative	28	39	−24	−35	2	7
Labour	−31	−39	28	39	−8	−8
Alliance	−1	−3	−1	−1	7	−1
Paper's partisanship	77	85	−73	−81	−13	−6

Notes: Bias coded +1 if favourable, −1 if unfavourable, 0 otherwise.

Electors' partisanship variables coded 1 if they preferred that party, 0 otherwise.

Papers' partisanship coded +1 if *Express, Mail, Sun, Star, Telegraph, The Times*; other papers coded −1; 0 if no paper.

It is difficult to compare the perceptions of Labour and Conservative identifiers who read the same paper since the numbers in our sample who read any one paper were low and tended to be drawn predominantly from one party or another. A breakdown is possible only for large-circulation papers like the *Sun* and the *Mirror*. Amongst *Mirror* readers, there was no difference between Labour and Conservative identifiers in their perception of the *Mirror*'s anti-Conservative bias, though Conservative *Mirror* readers were somewhat less likely to detect a pro-Labour bias. Amongst *Sun* readers, there was little difference between Labour and Conservative identifiers in their perceptions of its anti-Labour, pro-Conservative bias. Both Labour and Conservative

TABLE 6.6. *Perceptions of Paper Bias by Readers' Party Identification* (%)

	Reader's own party identification	Net perceptions of positive bias	
		FF	SF
About Conservatives	Con	51	58
	Lab	−16	−30
	Alln	22	15
About Labour	Con	−39	−51
	Lab	22	32
	Alln	−20	−20
About Alliance	Con	−24	−26
	Lab	−30	−41
	Alln	−20	−33

Note: Net perceptions of bias defined as for table 6.1.

Sun readers increasingly alleged pro-Conservative bias in the *Sun* as the campaign drew to a close.

Another approach is to group together the readers of various right-wing papers and contrast them with readers of left-wing papers. We can look at the relationship between perceptions of paper bias and the electors' own partisanship amongst 'readers of right-wing papers', though it has to be remembered that different voters are evaluating different individual papers. Despite that problem, the results clearly confirm our conclusion that paper readers did not react against the partisanship of their papers, they gloried in it. Conservatives who read right-wing papers saw *more* pro-Conservative bias in these papers than Labour identifiers who read the same set of right-wing papers. Labour identifiers who read left-wing papers saw *more* pro-Labour bias in these papers than Conservatives who read the same set of papers (Table 6.8).

In partisan terms, people reacted *against* television news, alleging antagonistic bias; but they reacted very differently towards the press. Ultimately, of course, those who find press bias offensive can change their newspaper, but the BBC is collective property and 'exit' is an inappropriate response.

PUBLIC PERCEPTIONS OF MEDIA USEFULNESS

In the week after the election we asked our panel to look back over the whole campaign and tell us how useful they had found television, the press, and other sources for: (1) helping decide what party leaders and personalities were really like; (2) keeping them informed about the issues; and (3) helping them decide

TABLE 6.7. *Perceptions of Television Bias by Viewers' Party Identification* (%)

	Viewers' own party identification	Net perceptions of positive bias	
		FF	SF
Perceptions of BBC bias			
About Conservatives	Con	−7	−12
	Lab	22	23
	Alln	12	12
About Labour	Con	5	14
	Lab	−16	−23
	Alln	−7	−6
About Alliance	Con	2	−2
	Lab	−10	−11
	Alln	−6	0
Perceptions of ITV bias			
About Conservatives	Con	2	−2
	Lab	6	8
	Alln	11	1
About Labour	Con	−1	7
	Lab	−4	−1
	Alln	−3	−4
About Alliance	Con	−1	−2
	Lab	−3	−3
	Alln	−3	−3

Notes: Net perceptions of bias defined as for Table 6.1.

Table restricted to those who had watched the appropriate channel on the day or day before the interview.

TABLE 6.8. *Perceptions of Paper Bias by Readers' and Papers'*
Partisanship (%)

	Reader's own party identification	Net perceptions of positive bias	
		FF	SF
Amongst readers of right-wing papers			
About Conservatives	Con	76	82
	Lab	67	78
	Alln	84	85
About Labour	Con	−61	−72
	Lab	−63	−75
	Alln	−75	−82
About Alliance	Con	−27	−27
	Lab	−53	−55
	Alln	−32	−52
Amongst readers of left-wing papers			
About Conservatives	Con	−76	−74
	Lab	−70	−83
	Alln	−76	−85
About Labour	Con	72	73
	Lab	75	85
	Alln	79	82
About Alliance	Con	−21	−14
	Lab	−20	−38
	Alln	−12	−38

Note: Net perceptions of bias defined as for Table 6.1.

how to vote. We asked respondents to assess the usefulness of each source for each purpose by giving it a 'mark out of ten'.

Across nine sources and three purposes the average mark awarded was 5.1, almost exactly half marks. 'Television generally' scored best with an average of 6.0, closely followed by BBC-TV news at 5.7 and ITV news at 5.5. Newspapers were not far behind with an average score of 5.3. Party Election Broadcasts on TV and radio scored 5.1. BBC Radio news scored 5.0 and Commercial Radio news 4.4. Party leaflets came bottom with 4.0 while conversations with family, friends, and acquaintances scored 4.8, which was better than party leaflets or Commercial Radio but worse than the press or television. Gunter, Svennevig and Wober (1986, p. 100), in their study of the 1983 election, also found that the public rated television the most useful, followed by the press, and then by personal conversations and radio news. Personal conversations are not independent of media news, however, since their content often consists of a review of information and opinion originally derived from the press or television. (See McLeod *et al.*, 1979, for some empirical evidence on the content of personal conversations.)

Taking the nine sources together, they scored best on informing electors about the issues (5.7), slightly less well on informing them about personalities (5.4), and very much worse on helping them decide how to vote (4.1). Every one of the nine sources was rated best for information on the issues and worst for helping people decide how to vote.

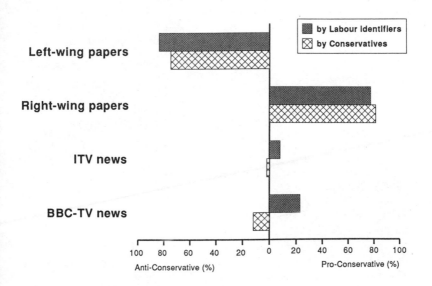

FIG. 6.2. Perceptions of Net Bias by Voters' Partisanship
(see Tables 6.7 and 6.8)

Moreover, the spread of scores was greatest on issue-information and least on vote-guidance. Comparing television with the press, for example, the public rated television a full 1.0 marks better than the press for providing issue-information, and 0.7 marks better on providing leader-information, but only 0.3 marks better for helping viewers and readers decide how to vote (Table 6.9). In Chapter 4 we recalled the well-established view that the British electorate came to rely more on television than the press from the late 1950s or early 1960s onwards. Our present findings qualify that conclusion. They suggest that in 1987 British electors relied much more heavily on television than the press for information, but only a little more for vote-guidance. There is some corroboration for our conclusion in previous research, however: at the 1983 election Gunter, Svennevig and Wober (1986, p. 119) found that 'whilst television clearly emerged from among various sources of information about politics as the major source, it seemed to be

TABLE 6.9. *Public Perceptions of Media Usefulness*
(average marks out of 10)

Source	For issue-information (a)	For leader-information (b)	For vote-guidance (c)	Average of (a), (b), and (c)	% who did not give rating
TV generally	7.1	6.3	4.5	6.0	3
BBC-TV news	6.6	6.1	4.4	5.7	8
ITV news	6.3	6.0	4.3	5.5	17
Newspapers	6.1	5.6	4.2	5.3	12
PEBs	5.6	5.5	4.1	5.1	13
BBC Radio news	5.6	5.4	3.9	5.0	39
Conversations	5.2	5.2	4.0	4.8	5
Commercial Radio news	4.8	4.7	3.6	4.4	61
Party leaflets	4.4	4.2	3.5	4.0	13
Average	5.7	5.4	4.1	5.1	

Notes: Average scores are based upon answers given by those willing and able to rate the source. Radio had a relatively small news audience.

This table is based upon all respondents to our Post-Election Wave of interviews. Subsequent tables are based upon the smaller number of respondents in our multi-wave panel.

relatively less important in the decision-making process of which way to vote'.

It may be a surprise to find that television enjoyed its greatest competitive advantage on issue-information. Surely television is the medium for getting to know personalities, but the press is the medium for a detailed understanding of the issues? Surely the detailed issue coverage in the *Guardian* and *The Times* must be superior to the necessarily brief and superficial coverage of issues on television? Perhaps that is so; but very few British newspaper readers read papers like the *Guardian* and *The Times*; most read tabloids such as the *Sun*, the *Star*, the *Mirror*, the *Express*, or the *Mail*. Against that competition it is not altogether surprising that British newspaper readers found better issue coverage on British television. Our image of the typical newspaper reader in Britain has to be that of someone reading a tabloid, not a highbrow quality paper.

WHO FOUND THE MEDIA USEFUL?

Some people found the media more useful than others. We used multiple regressions to gauge the influence upon media usefulness-ratings of: political interest and discussion, different motivations for following the campaign, social and political background factors, perceptions of bias, and the intellectual weight of the press. In addition we used voters' degree of preference for their first-choice party (over their second choice) as yet another potential influence upon their ratings of the media's usefulness.

The main influences on usefulness-ratings were people's interest in politics and their motivations for following the campaign. Their degree of preference for one party over others had an important influence upon the usefulness-ratings they gave the media for helping them decide how to vote (those with clear preferences found the media less useful for that purpose) but had little or no influence on other aspects of usefulness-ratings. Surprisingly, perceptions of bias never had a significant impact on usefulness-ratings.

The factors influencing ratings given to television for providing information on personalities and issues were almost identical to each other. For both purposes, television scored significantly higher amongst those who found politics interesting at the end of the campaign, amongst information-seekers, and amongst those who read lowbrow tabloids. With minor variations the same factors influenced their ratings of both BBC and ITV.

But the factors influencing ratings given to television for helping people decide how to vote were different. Once again, motivations were a key factor but it was vote-guidance seekers, not information seekers, who now rated television most highly. Since that showed a degree of consistency in attitudes, it was not entirely unexpected. More surprising was the relationship with political interest. Television scored best on helping people decide how to vote if they found politics interesting during the campaign but had lacked a general interest in politics in the mid-term. Television therefore helped make up the minds of those who were *newly interested* in politics, or *unusually interested* in politics, interested in the election campaign but not very interested in politics more generally.

Ratings of radio news were less predictable than ratings of television but they too were influenced by recent political interest, motivations for following the campaign, and degree of party preference. Once again, perceptions of bias had no influence.

Similar factors explain newspaper ratings also. Those who found politics interesting in the campaign but had *not* been interested in politics a year earlier gave the press high ratings for helping them decide how to vote. Vote-guidance seekers found both the press and television specially useful for making up their mind how to vote. But information seekers did not rate the press, unlike television, particularly highly for providing information. Conversely, reinforcement seekers found the press, unlike television, specially useful, at least for providing information about personalities.

The most surprising influence on press ratings is, however, the one that is *not* there. Multiple regression analysis suggests that readers did not find the highbrow press significantly more useful than the lowbrow press for any purpose: reading a highbrow paper had no influence in the multiple regressions for newspaper 'usefulness' (Table 6.10).

Those who read highbrow papers found their papers no more useful for helping them decide how to vote or for revealing politicians' personalities, and only a little more useful for ex-

T_A_R_L_E 6.10. *Multiple Regression Analyses of the Usefulness of Television and Newspapers*

	Television generally			Newspapers		
	L	I	V	L	I	V
Interest (MID)	•	•	−12	•	•	−18
Interest (FF)	•	22	•	19	20	23
Interest (SF)	22	•	16	•	•	•
Discussion (PRE)	•	•	•	−15	•	•
Highbrow paper (MID)	−17	−17	•	•	•	•
Reinforcement	•	•	•	15	•	•
Guidance	•	•	27	•	•	13
Information	19	18	•	•	•	•
Preference (FF)	•	•	−19	•	•	−18
RSQ	13	12	18	7	4	13

Notes: Analysis by forward stepwise regression, entering blocks of predictors in the following sequence: interest, discussion, type of paper, motivations for following the campaign, perceptions of bias, socio-economic background, ideology, strength of partisanship, and degree of preference for one party. Where a predictor was measured in several waves, each of the measurements was used as a potential predictor in the stepwise regression.

A dot indicates that a predictor proved statistically insignificant. Predictors that never proved significant have been excluded from the table.

plaining political issues. Reading the highbrow press clearly made readers somewhat disdainful towards television news and Party Election Broadcasts, but not much more enthusiastic about the press. Of course, different kinds of people read different papers. Those who read the highbrow press would probably have found the lowbrow tabloids woefully inadequate, but those who read the tabloids would probably have found the highbrow press too complex, long-winded, repetitive, waffling, and boring to be useful. Our survey shows that highbrow readers rated their papers no more useful *for them* than the lowbrow papers were *for their readers* (Table 6.11).

TABLE 6.11. *How Newspaper Readers Rated the Usefulness of Television and Newspapers* (average marks out of 10)

Source	Readers		
	Lowbrow	Middlebrow	Highbrow
TV generally	6.3	6.1	5.3
BBC-TV news	5.9	5.8	5.1
ITV news	5.7	5.7	4.7
PEBs	5.3	5.2	4.1
Newspapers	5.1	5.3	5.3

Note: Figures are the average rating of the source as useful on the issues, on the leaders, and for voting choice.

By comparing the usefulness-ratings each respondent gave to television and the press we can see how many people found television more useful than the press, how many found the press more useful than television, and how many found them equally useful. Given that usefulness was rated on an eleven-point scale

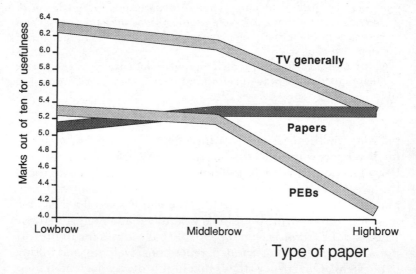

FIG. 6.3. Usefulness of News Sources by Newspaper Readership (see Table 6.11)

(0 to 10) we might expect that relatively few would rate television and the press exactly equal. Alternatively, we might feel that people who took care to give different media sources exactly the same rating on an eleven-point scale were indicating quite *strongly* that they found them equally useful.

By a majority of 56 per cent to 22 per cent, citizens found television more useful than the press for providing issue-information (a further 22 per cent found them equally useful). By a smaller majority of 48 per cent to 30 per cent, they found television more useful than the press for providing information about party leaders (with 22 per cent, once again, rating the two sources equally useful). But on helping them decide how to vote, opinion was much more evenly divided: 36 per cent preferred television, 24 per cent the press, and a remarkable 40 per cent said the two sources were equally useful (Table 6.12).

TABLE 6.12. *Relative Usefulness of Press and Television* (%)

	For issue-information				For leader-information				For vote-guidance			
	TV	=	P	(TV−P)	TV	=	P	(TV−P)	TV	=	P	(TV−P)
All electors	56	22	22	(34)	48	22	30	(18)	36	40	24	(12)
readers of												
No paper	65	22	13	(52)	63	15	22	(41)	55	34	12	(43)
Sun/Star	67	21	12	(55)	53	21	26	(27)	35	41	25	(10)
Mirror	57	22	22	(35)	38	31	31	(7)	32	49	19	(13)
Express/Mail	48	29	23	(25)	37	27	36	(1)	32	37	30	(2)
Telegraph etc.	45	22	33	(12)	33	25	42	(−9)	23	56	20	(3)
Guardian	16	28	57	(−41)	36	20	43	(−7)	15	42	43	(−28)

Notes: TV means % who rated TV higher than press; = means % who rated TV and press equally; P means % who rated press higher than TV; (TV−P) means % who preferred TV *minus* % who preferred press: it measures the preference for television rather than the press.

Readers defined as those who were regular readers (three times a week) of the same paper (or group of papers) in the spring of 1986 and the spring of 1987.

'*Telegraph* etc.' stands for *Telegraph* or *The Times* or *Financial Times*.

For providing issue-information, persistent readers of the *Sun* or *Star* preferred television to the press by 67 per cent to 12 per cent: a majority of 55 per cent. *Sun/Star* readers' preference for

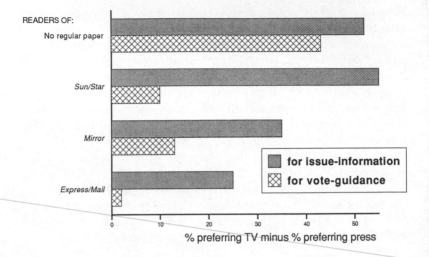

FIG. 6.4. Relative Usefulness of Tabloids and Television by Newspaper
Readership (see Table 6.12)

television as a source of issue-information was just as great as
that of people who did not read any paper regularly. Next came
Mirror readers, who preferred television to the press by a majority
of 35 per cent, and *Express/Mail* readers, who preferred television
by a majority of 25 per cent. *Telegraph/Times* readers were more
ambivalent, however, and our small sample of *Guardian* readers
preferred the press by a big majority.

On balance, people also preferred television rather than the
press as a source of information about political leaders. But
despite its video pictorial qualities, and its much vaunted 'personal' contact with party leaders, television's advantage over the
press in giving information about leaders was less than its
advantage on issue-information. Perhaps television was just too
obsequious towards leaders to be revealing. Overall a majority of
34 per cent preferred television for issue-information, while a
majority of only 18 per cent preferred television for information
about leaders. Those who did not read a particular paper regularly,
and those who read the *Sun* or *Star*, showed a clear preference for
television on leader-information; but readers of other papers
were divided on whether the press or television was best.

When it came to deciding how to vote however, the most frequent response was that television and the press were equally useful. People who were not regular paper readers relied more on television, while *Guardian* readers relied more on the press; but a plurality of every other paper's readers said they found press and television equally useful. So amongst tabloid readers generally, but especially amongst *Sun/Star* readers, there was a dramatic difference between their overwhelming preference for television as a source of information and their reliance upon both press and television for helping them decide how to vote.

We might have expected that people would give particularly low ratings to sources they described as biased but there was little evidence of any such reaction. Most people thought their newspapers were biased and very few thought ITV news was biased. Yet newspapers and PEBs scored only marginally lower than ITV news on usefulness. More thought BBC-TV news was biased yet it scored marginally higher than ITV news on all three aspects of usefulness.

At the individual level, too, those who perceived bias on television news rated it only very slightly less useful than those who did not, while those who perceived bias in their papers rated their papers slightly *more* useful than those who did not (Table 6.13). Perceptions of media bias never proved statistically significant in any of our multiple regressions predicting useful-ness-ratings.

TABLE 6.13. *How Perceptions of Bias Affected Ratings for Usefulness* (average mark out of 10)

Source	Rating by those who perceive the source to be					
	Unbiased about Con	Biased about Con	Unbiased about Lab	Biased about Lab	Unbiased about Alln	Biased about Alln
BBC-TV	6.0	5.5	5.9	5.5	5.9	5.9
Papers	5.1	5.5	5.4	5.4	5.4	5.4

Note: 'Biased about' includes both bias towards the party and bias against the party.

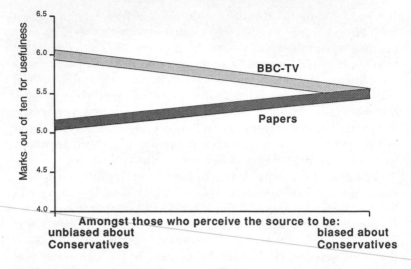

FIG. 6.5. Perceived Bias and Usefulness (see Table 6.13)

WHO FOUND ALTERNATIVES TO MASS MEDIA NEWS USEFUL?

Party Election Broadcasts (PEBs) at election-time and the equivalent Party Political Broadcasts (PPBs) at non-election times are
one method by which broadcasting attempts to achieve balance
and impartiality between the parties. The parties themselves
control the content. In one sense they are the British equivalent
of political advertising on American television, but they differ
from such advertising in three very important ways: first, PEB
broadcasting is free (although the parties have to bear at least
some of the production costs—indeed, all of the production costs
if they wish to use private production facilities); second, the
number of PEB broadcasts is fixed by agreement between broadcasters and the parties to reflect (roughly) the current popular
standing of the parties (in 1987 Labour, the Liberal–SDP Alliance,
and the Conservatives got exactly equal time for PEBs while
other parties received very much less); third, the broadcasters
have insisted, against the politicians' wishes, that PEBs be short
programmes typically ten minutes long, rather than high-impact
adverts of perhaps twenty or thirty seconds' duration. While the
politicians see PEBs as a device for party propaganda, the broad-

casters see PEBs as a platform for parties to inform the electorate by stating their case rather than chanting their slogans. Our panel rated PEBs much lower than the press or television news for providing information on issues, but similar to the press for providing information on leaders, and close behind the press and television news for helping them decide how to vote. Wober (1989a) presents evidence to suggest that electors find mid-term PPBs, especially opposition PPBs, much more useful than PEBs during the campaign. During the final campaign, voters hardly need such contrived devices as PEBs to find out about the issues and personalities in party debate, but during the mid-term there is so much concentration on government actions and personalities that PPBs play a much more significant role in publicizing opposition policies and personalities. At all times, electors find PPBs or PEBs very much more useful than party leaflets.

The most predictable usefulness ratings were those for PEBs. Those with a recent interest in politics, who found the election interesting but did not have a general interest in politics at other times, gave PEBs high ratings for usefulness on leaders, issues, and voting choice. The same people also found party leaflets particularly useful. Lowbrow tabloid readers gave PEBs high ratings for all three purposes. Reinforcement seekers gave PEBs high ratings for providing information about party leaders while vote-guidance seekers gave both PEBs and party leaflets high ratings on issues and voting choice. Young voters found party leaflets more useful than older voters (Table 6.14).

Those who found the election campaign interesting gave personal conversations high ratings for all purposes. Information seekers found personal conversations useful for gaining information about leaders and issues. Vote-guidance seekers, and those who lacked strong preferences, found personal conversations useful in helping them decide how to vote. People who discussed politics more during the campaign gave personal conversations a somewhat higher rating for providing information on the issues, but not for other purposes. Indeed, frequency of discussion had remarkably little influence on usefulness-ratings for personal conversations, less influence than motivations, for example. Clearly, quantity did not necessarily imply quality (Table 6.15).

TABLE 6.14. *Multiple Regression Analyses of the Usefulness of Party Election Broadcasts and Party Leaflets*

	PEBs			Leaflets		
	L	I	V	L	I	V
Interest (MID)	−18	−18	−15	−17	·	−17
Interest (FF)	19	24	25	·	·	14
Interest (SF)	12	·	·	17	·	·
Highbrow paper (MID)	−14	−13	−15	·	·	·
Reinforcement	15	·	·	·	·	·
Guidance	·	17	21	·	13	15
Preference (PRE)	·	·	·	·	·	−15
Preference (FF)	·	·	−15	·	·	·
RSQ	15	13	18	5	2	10

Notes: For notes on the regression and the meaning of the dot see Table 6.10.

TABLE 6.15. *Multiple Regression Analyses of the Usefulness of Personal Conversations*

	For leader-information	For issue-information	For vote-guidance
Interest (MID)	·	·	−12
Interest (FF)	·	·	21
Interest (SF)	15	11	·
Discussion (SF)	·	15	·
Guidance	·	·	18
Information	17	15	·
Preference (PRE)	·	·	−14
RSQ	7	9	11

Notes: For notes on the regression and the meaning of the dot see Table 6.10.

CONCLUSIONS

Academic analysts are unanimous that the British press is highly partisan, even if it is less so than it was in the last century and even though proprietors are strongly profit-motivated. It seems to have become more stridently partisan in the 1970s and 1980s than it was in the 1960s. Three-quarters of all newspaper readers in our panel agreed that the papers they had read on the day of the interview were biased in their coverage of the Conservative and Labour Parties, though less than half said their papers gave biased coverage of the Alliance. Tabloid readers were more likely to allege bias than highbrow readers, particularly in the closing stages of the campaign, though differences between them were initially quite small. On balance, newspaper readers agreed with academic analysts about the direction of bias.

In contrast, political scientists have usually claimed that television news is unbiased (though sociologists have been more sceptical). Our content analysis of television during the election campaign seems to suggest that television was biased towards the right wing and, separately, towards the government of the day. Our survey panel shows that about a quarter of the electorate thought BBC-TV news was biased in its treatment of the Conservative government, though rather less felt it was biased in its treatment of other parties. Only one in seven thought ITV news was biased in its treatment of the Conservatives and, again, rather less felt it was biased in its treatment of other parties. On balance, people felt the bias on both channels favoured the Conservative Party and the Conservative Party alone.

Age, education, ideology, even strength of partisanship, had little influence on perceptions of bias on television or in the press. Perceptions of bias were also unrelated to motivations for following the campaign or interest in politics during the campaign itself. However, those who had expressed a more general interest in politics during the parliamentary mid-term were more likely to allege bias on television and in their papers during the campaign.

The direction of alleged bias was influenced in a complex way by the critics' own partisanship. People tended to see television as biased against their own party while they thought their paper was biased towards their own party. No doubt they chose their paper partly with that bias in mind while they felt that television bias was being inflicted upon them against their will. The correlation between being Conservative and alleging *anti*-Conservative bias on BBC-TV rose from 24 per cent in the first fortnight of the campaign to 32 per cent in the second. By contrast, the correlation between voters being Conservative and alleging *pro*-Conservative bias in their newspaper rose from 28 per cent in the first fortnight of the campaign to 39 per cent in the second. Perceptions of newspaper bias depended more, however, on the partisanship of the paper being read than on the partisanship of the reader who read it. None the less, Conservatives who read right-wing papers saw *more* pro-Conservative bias in these papers than Labour identifiers who read the same set of right-wing papers.

We might have expected that those who alleged bias on television or in their paper would be reluctant to describe that source as useful but there was little evidence of any such reaction. Voters' assessments of media usefulness varied more with their political interest, and in a complex way. Television, newspapers, PEBs, party leaflets, and personal conversations were all most useful in helping people decide how to vote if they found politics interesting during the campaign but had lacked a more general interest in politics in the mid-term. The media helped to make up the minds of those who were *newly interested* in politics, or *unusually interested* in politics, interested in the election but not very interested in politics generally.

People rated television the most useful source of information about party leaders and political issues, and the most helpful source for making up their minds how to vote. BBC-TV news scored best, followed by ITV news, newspapers, PEBs, personal conversations, and lastly radio news. (For most listeners, radio news was not the high-quality, in-depth BBC Radio 4 news, but BBC Radios 1 and 2 news inserts, or Commercial Radio news.) Every one of these nine sources was rated better for providing information than for helping people decide how to vote.

Although the public preferred television to the press for all purposes, they preferred television most of all for providing information about the issues. For deciding how to vote, however, only a small plurality preferred television and 40 per cent of voters said they found television and the press equally useful.

Readers of the tabloid press overwhelmingly preferred television rather than the press as an information source but, like other voters, they had a relatively slight preference for television rather than the press for helping them decide how to vote.

Surprisingly, readers of the highbrow press found their papers scarcely any more useful than readers of the lowbrow press. Reading the highbrow press made people somewhat disdainful towards television, but no more enthusiastic about the press. Conversely, the reason why readers of the lowbrow press had such strong preferences for television news was not that they were particularly dissatisified with their papers but that they were particularly enthusiastic about the quality of television.

7

Media Influence on Perceptions of Politics

The apparently simple question 'Does the media influence voters?' is too general to be meaningful. At the very least it prompts the response 'What elements of the media? What influence?' We need to distinguish between different media sources, and also between the media's ability to inform and its ability to persuade. Different elements of the media perform different functions. From what we know about their audience and their content, we would expect major differences between the influence of television and the influence of the press, and major differences also between the influence of highbrow and lowbrow sources. If they have any influence at all, different media sources should influence their audiences in different ways.

THE EXPECTED INFLUENCE OF TELEVISION

Television news has three significant characteristics that affect its ability to influence the electorate. First, it is pervasive. Nearly everyone watches television news regularly. Second, it is relatively undifferentiated. Three-quarters of the 1987 electorate said they regularly watched both BBC-TV and ITV news. In addition, our analysis of television news content showed that BBC and ITV news are very similar anyway. Third, it is relatively unbiased. Despite our finding that television news is biased, there is no doubt that it is less biased than the press, and that such bias as there is on television is in the same direction on both BBC and ITV.

Given those characteristics we should not expect BBC and ITV viewers to be influenced in different ways. Whatever influence television news has on voters, it would be likely to affect all, or nearly all voters. It would not affect different audiences in different ways. If we seek evidence of television's influence, we should correlate general trends in public opinion with trends in the content of television news. Moreover, despite its failings, British television is still very much an information medium rather than a propaganda medium. So we should expect it to have a stronger influence on public information and perceptions than on public attitudes and choices.

THE EXPECTED INFLUENCE OF THE PRESS

The press is entirely different. First, it is not so pervasive. Second, it is highly differentiated. While most people regularly watch both BBC and ITV news, few read more than one morning newspaper. Indeed there are so many newspapers in contrast to the two television networks, that relatively few voters (as a percentage) read even the best-selling paper. In addition, analyses of press coverage show that their content varies enormously. Third, the press is partisan, biased, and proud of it. The press always has been a medium of propaganda as well as a medium of information. Particular papers vary in the degree to which they emphasize propaganda rather than information, and this emphasis also varies through time. In the final 1987 election campaign the press became more partisan and its emphasis on propaganda increased. The tabloids in particular carried relatively little in-depth information but a lot of propaganda. So we should expect readers of different papers to be influenced in different directions depending upon the content of their own particular papers. We should expect the mass-selling tabloid press to have a stronger influence on public attitudes and choices than on public information and perceptions. Highbrow papers might be more like television, primarily affecting their readers' information and perceptions.

PERCEPTIONS AND ATTITUDES

At first it seems that we can draw a sharp distinction between perceptions and attitudes. Attitudes involve preferences, choices, evaluations, approval, or disapproval, while perceptions do not. Perceptions are simply a vision of political realities. Whether people like or dislike what they see is a matter of attitudes, not perceptions. Perceptions need not be strictly accurate. Different people may have different perceptions of politics. Some may be more aware, more knowledgeable, than others. Some may be misinformed because they misread their newspaper, or because their paper prints inaccurate information, or even because they do not believe what is printed in their paper. Perceptions are not the same thing as knowledge, but they are what the holder of the perception believes to be knowledge. Perceptions contain no element of approval or disapproval though they may trigger a reaction in terms of approval. When someone notices the Chancellor's announcement of a tax cut that is a perception; when they approve or disapprove, that is an attitude.

Unfortunately this clear conceptual distinction between perceptions and attitudes is unrealistic. In practice there is a continuum ranging from pure value-free perceptions at one end to pure choice at the other. Towards the pure perception end of the spectrum is awareness of opinion polls, awareness of local constituency candidates, awareness of campaign activities by party leaders, and awareness of the parties' campaign themes.

At the other extreme, the pure choice end of the spectrum, are explicit statements of choice, preference, approval, or disapproval: which party people think is best on economic matters for themselves and their families, for Britain as a whole, or for the unemployed; their evaluations of how well each party has handled issues like unemployment, inflation, defence, health, education, and social services; how warm they feel towards parties and their leaders; whether the parties should change their leaders or their policies, or both; and, last but not least, voting preferences.

In the middle of the spectrum, however, are perceptions with more than a hint of approval or disapproval implicit in them: perceptions of each party's electoral chances; perceptions of whether national economic performance and prospects are improving or declining; and images of the parties and party leaders. It is not at all obvious whether viewing party leaders as 'energetic' or 'decisive' is a perception or an attitude. To a foreign correspondent covering the British election for a foreign audience, whether a party leader appears energetic or decisive is simply a matter of objective reporting: a perception. To British voters, especially those who identify strongly with a political party, 'energetic' or 'decisive' probably imply approval: for them, images are at the margin between perceptions and attitudes.

Media influence on perceptions is likely to depend upon whether they are at the pure perception end of the spectrum or at the margin between perceptions and attitudes. Sheer information can be boosted quickly by a media blitz, or by individuals' personal information-gathering resources—their education, their interest and involvement with politics, and their use of information-rich highbrow news sources. By contrast, perceptions that verge on being attitudes are likely to be more resistant to change and more dependent upon individuals' partisan backgrounds—their pre-existing sense of party identification, and their use of partisan news sources such as right-wing (or left-wing) papers.

This chapter uses two techniques to investigate media influence. To assess the impact of pervasive and consensual television news we can correlate trends in television news content and trends in overall public perceptions. To assess the impact of more differentiated media sources we can look for differences between their different audiences: differences between readers of highbrow or lowbrow papers, for example, or between readers of right-wing and left-wing papers.

THE IMPACT OF A CHANGING TELEVISION CONSENSUS

Our analysis of television news content in Chapter 4 showed that controversy reached a peak on television in the third week of the campaign. Both BBC-TV and ITV, both early and main evening news, all followed the same trend: they all screened more presentation than controversy until the third week; then they screened between two and four times as much controversy as presentation in the third week, before reverting to more presentation at the end of the campaign. On television the campaign very clearly reached a climax in the third week (25–9 May).

But all that controversy on television failed to excite the public. The frequency of political discussions rose sharply between the pre-campaign week and the final campaign, but then it continued to rise steadily throughout the campaign to peak at the very end. The number of voters who found what was happening in politics 'very interesting' dropped sharply between our pre-campaign week (when Thatcher was in Moscow and Kinnock newly returned from Washington) and the campaign itself. During the final campaign interest sagged, if anything, though there was really very little trend. So the tremendous burst of controversy in the third week of television's campaign coverage failed to stimulate either grass-roots discussion or public interest. In that respect television had no influence (Table 7.1).

TABLE 7.1. *Trends in Television Controversy and Public Reactions* (%)

	Pre-campaign	Campaign week				
		1	2	3	4	5
TV news (headlines only)						
Controversy	9	14	18	41	22	16
Voters						
Discuss politics often	19	30	32	33	36	41
Find politics very interesting	26	18	16	17	15	17

Note: For a definition of our measure of controversy on television news see Chapter 4, Table 4.2.

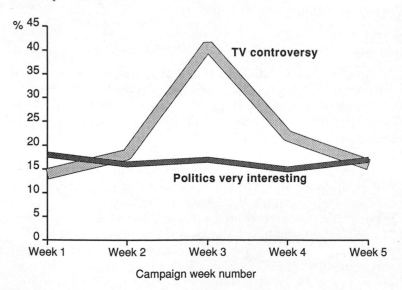

FIG. 7.1. TV Controversy and Voters' Political Interest (see Table 7.1)

One of the classic findings of media research in British election campaigns is Trenaman and McQuail's (1961) assertion that 'the evidence strongly suggests that people *think about what they are told . . . but at no level do they think what* they are told'. This is usually called the 'agenda-setting function of the media'. (The term 'agenda-setting' was popularized by McCombs and Shaw, 1972; Shaw and McCombs, 1977; though the idea had been around since at least Lazarsfeld, Berelson, and Gaudet, 1944. For a producers' rather than a consumers' perspective on agenda-setting see Hetherington, 1985; Blumler and Gurevitch, 1986; Blumler, Gurevitch, and Nossiter, 1986 and 1989.)

This agenda-setting thesis is very plausible and usually treated as an established law of social science in introductory textbooks, though much more sceptically in research reports. But, as McQuail (1987, pp. 275–6) himself has recently pointed out, most of the accumulated evidence is inconclusive and the media-dominated agenda-setting hypothesis has 'the status of a plausible but unproven idea'. Studies by McLeod, Becker, and Byrnes (1974) and Iyengar and Kinder (1987), for example, suggest that the media set the agenda for only a part of their audience: those highly reliant on a particular news source, those low in political involvement and information, and those who are relatively *in*attentive to the news generally—in short, those who are marginal to politics.

How did the trends in television's news agenda compare with trends in the electorate's agenda in 1987? Chapter 4 showed that television's issue agenda was generally biased towards security issues when compared with the electorate's own agenda. But perhaps television edged closer to the public, or the public edged closer to television, as the campaign progressed?

Unemployment came top of the list of issues that the public thought the parties 'should be' talking about (see Table 7.2) Throughout the first two weeks of the campaign almost two-thirds of our panel cited unemployment as the 'main issue' that should be discussed but it got little coverage on television news. In the first week of the campaign over half our panel felt Labour was addressing the issue, but under one-third thought that about the Alliance and only one-fifth about the Conservative Party. According to our panel all three parties, including Labour, seemed to drift away from the issue as the campaign progressed.

TABLE 7.2. *Trends in Media and Public Agendas* (%)

	Pre-campaign	Campaign week				
		1	2	3	4	5
UNEMPLOYMENT						
TV election news	3	4	12	3	9	1
Voters' perceptions of parties						
Conservatives	13	20	15	11	10	7
Labour	52	54	55	49	46	35
Alliance	35	29	28	24	24	21
Voters' own views						
'Should be discussed'	51	66	63	56	57	56
'Extremely important'	49	64	65	61	65	63
INFLATION						
TV election news	0	0	1	1	0	1
Voters' perceptions of parties						
Conservatives	21	16	11	6	7	5
Labour	1	2	1	0	0	1
Alliance	2	1	0	0	1	3
Voters' own views						
'Should be discussed'	6	3	2	2	2	3
'Extremely important'	33	41	43	40	46	44
HEALTH/EDUCATION/SOCIAL SERVICES						
TV election news	6	3	13	14	10	6
Voters' perceptions of parties						
Conservatives	5	6	8	15	9	8
Labour	11	14	10	13	20	32
Alliance	14	5	7	10	18	17
Voters' own views						
'Should be discussed'	20	16	16	17	17	18
'Extremely important'	60	77	77	77	76	77
DEFENCE						
TV election news	35	5	12	26	3	3
Voters' perceptions of parties						
Conservatives	40	3	13	39	45	46
Labour	21	4	7	17	15	14
Alliance	11	2	8	16	12	14
Voters' own views						
'Should be discussed'	7	3	6	11	12	10
'Extremely important'	39	42	46	49	50	48

So neither television nor the parties moved closer to the electorate on unemployment: they moved away from the electorate, increasingly avoiding an issue the public wanted to discuss.

Did the electorate follow the parties and the media? Our panel gave more weight to unemployment throughout the final campaign than they had done in the Pre-Campaign wave. They never wavered in describing the issue as extremely important for their voting decision: 64 per cent called it extremely important in the first week and 63 per cent in the last. On the other hand, when television coverage of unemployment almost ceased in the third week, public demand for political debate on the issue also dropped slightly, from 66 per cent to 56 per cent, and it remained at this new lower level thereafter. So on unemployment there is some evidence of a slight tendency for the public to follow the lead of the parties and the media but it was a very slight adjustment of public attitudes.

Inflation was the scourge of the mid-1970s but not the mid-1980s. Throughout the campaign less than 3 per cent of voters said it was the main issue that should be discussed. Very few television news items, less than 1 per cent, focused on inflation. Labour and the Alliance seemed to ignore the issue. At the start of the campaign people thought it was the main issue being stressed by the Conservatives, but they soon changed their minds. On inflation, the Conservative Party seemed to fall into line with television, the other parties, and the public.

Health, education, and social services were issues that came second only to unemployment in terms of public priorities. In terms of professed influence on their voting decisions, people rated them far more important even than unemployment. Yet television paid relatively little attention to them. Fully 77 per cent of our panel throughout the campaign rated these issues as 'extremely important' for their voting choice, but television news gave them less coverage than defence, though more than unemployment and inflation.

On these issues the parties moved towards the concerns of the electorate. At the start only 14 per cent of our panel reported Labour stressing these issues, but the figure rose to 20 per cent in the fourth week and 32 per cent in the fifth as Labour sought to divert attention away from defence and to move on from unemployment, which directly affected only a small minority, to education and especially the National Health Service, which directly affected the vast majority of the electorate. According to our panel, the Alliance also switched towards a greater emphasis on health, education, and social services. The number of voters who cited social issues as their top priority, or who claimed such issues were 'extremely important' to their voting decision, hardly varied at all throughout the campaign. So on health, education, and social services there is no evidence that the public followed an agenda laid down by television or the parties. Quite the opposite. The enormous importance people attached to these issues seems eventually to have encouraged the parties to address them though it failed to encourage very much television coverage. On social issues the public's agenda influenced the party agenda if not the television agenda.

During our Pre-Campaign Wave in March defence was the main issue on television, the main issue stressed by the Conservative Party, and second only to unemployment as Labour's main issue. It could hardly have been otherwise when Thatcher and Kinnock were visiting Moscow and Washington to discuss Britain's defence policy. None the less, even in that week only 39 per cent of the electorate rated it 'extremely important' and a mere 7 per cent said it was the main issue that 'should be' discussed by the parties.

In the first week of the campaign only 5 per cent of television's election news focused on defence, only 3 per cent of the electorate thought the parties were stressing the issue, and only 3 per cent wished them to do so. The importance attached to every other issue rose sharply when the campaign opened but the importance attached to defence hardly changed.

But in the second week television coverage of defence doubled to 12 per cent, and in the third week it doubled again to 26 per cent before almost disappearing from the bulletins in the fourth and fifth weeks. The number of voters who felt the Conservative Party was stressing defence as its main theme rose from 3 per cent in the first week to 39 per cent in the third and 46 per cent by the end of the campaign. By the third week around 17 per cent thought Labour and the Alliance were also concentrating on defence.

If party rhetoric and television coverage ever set the public's agenda, they should have done so on defence. The switch from almost ignoring the issue in the first week to so much concentration in the third should have had some effect upon the public. And it did. But how much? The number of voters citing defence as the main issue they wished to see discussed by the parties rose from 3 per cent at the start of the campaign to only 11 per cent in the third week and then stabilized at that level. The number who cited defence as 'extremely important' for their voting decision rose from 42 per cent at the start to only 49 per cent in the third week and then it also stabilized at that level. So we can quantify the agenda-setting power of television and the parties during the campaign. By their enormous concentration on defence they raised the issue by just 8 per cent in terms of public priorities and by just 7 per cent in terms of electoral significance. It took an enormous amount of television coverage to produce only a small change in the public agenda (Table 7.2).

Towards the end of the campaign television focused more upon the two-party Labour versus Conservative battle and public expectations about Alliance performance declined. Did television

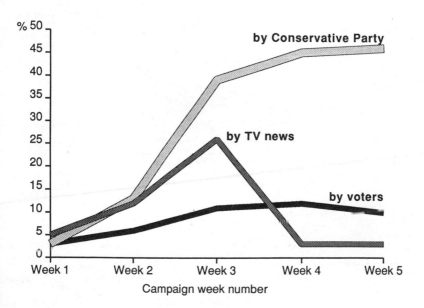

FIG. 7.2. The Emphasis on Defence by Voters, TV News, and the
Conservative Party (see Table 7.2)

marginalize the Alliance and thereby contribute to its failure? Television certainly did marginalize the Alliance, but there is no evidence that the bias in television coverage influenced the expectations of the electorate. Indeed the expectations of the electorate closely followed their awareness of opinion poll findings and ran ahead of the trends in television bias.

In the first week of the campaign only 44 per cent of the public felt Labour was a clear second in the opinion polls and as many as 19 per cent said the Alliance was running second. But perceptions that the Alliance was running second in the polls collapsed in the second week; and voters' assessment of Alliance chances of winning a majority or even holding the balance of power dropped sharply in the third week; while television's sharp switch to focus on the two-party Labour versus Conservative battle occurred in the fourth week. This time sequence is conclusive. Television bias was not the cause of declining expectations of Alliance success: it was a consequence of declining expectations amongst both journalists and the public at large (Table 7.3).

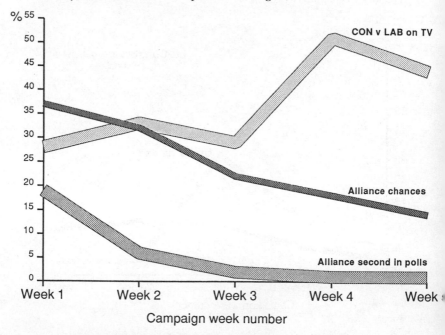

FIG. 7.3. Marginalizing the Alliance (see Table 7.3)

TABLE 7.3. *Trends in Television Coverage and Public Perceptions of Party Credibility* (%)

	Campaign week				
	1	2	3	4	5
Television coverage					
Con *v.* Lab (as % of controversy items)	28	33	29	51	44
Govt in action (as % of presentation items)	11	6	24	37	27
'Govt in action' *plus* 'Con' *minus* 'Lab' (as % of presentation items)	28	13	15	43	37
Voters' perceptions					
Con chances of majority 'very good'	75	71	64	59	65
Lab chances 'very good or some'	38	54	58	61	55
Alln chances 'very good or some'	37	32	22	18	14
Alln has chance of holding balance of power in hung parliament	40	41	35	34	30
Seen opinion polls and, in them:					
— Lab second	44	61	64	73	75
— Alln second	19	6	2	1	1
— second party close behind top party	25	31	36	44	43

Notes: For definitions of party presentation items and party controversy items on television news, see Chapter 4.

Almost everyone consistently thought the Conservatives had at least 'some' chance of winning a majority.

Relative coverage of Labour and Conservative was always biased towards the Conservative government but the degree of bias increased sharply (it tripled) in the fourth week of the campaign. Yet public perceptions of Conservative chances of victory sank to a minimum in that fourth week and assessments of Labour chances reached a peak then. (Though Conservative chances were always rated much higher than Labour's.) Once again the weight of television coverage had no effect on party credibility (though the nature of the coverage may have done so).

Public perceptions of party unity increased between our Pre-Campaign Wave and the start of the final campaign. During the pre-campaign week we recorded no items on television news which positively projected the image of party unity. These rather artificial news items were very much the product of the final election campaign. In public perceptions the gap between Conservative unity and Labour unity narrowed sharply in the first few days of the campaign and again at the end, but actually increased very slightly in the third week. That trend matches the trend in television projections of party unity, which were more favourable to Labour at the start and end of the campaign, but more favourable to the Conservatives in the middle, especially so in the third week. This does seem to be an area in which television coverage influenced public perceptions (Table 7.4).

TABLE 7.4. *Projections and Perceptions of Party Unity*

	Campaign week				
	1	2	3	4	5
Television coverage					
Positive image of Con unity *minus* image of Lab unity (%)	−2	7	11	7	−7
Voters' perceptions					
Mark out of ten for Con appearing united *minus* mark for Lab appearing united	2.4	1.5	1.6	1.1	0.9

Note: For definitions of television items projecting party unity, see Chapter 4.

There was a precipitous decline in television's projection of the Conservative Party's overall credibility in the fourth week of the campaign, a week that included the infamous 'wobbly Thursday' (see Chapter 4, Table 4.16, for details). But although it clearly had dramatic effects on the nerves of Conservative Central Office there is no evidence of any major shift in voting intentions at that time. Adverse contextualizing comments on television news did not set an anti-Conservative bandwagon rolling in the electorate, despite the fears of Conservative strategists.

NON-CONSENSUAL INFLUENCES ON POLITICAL PERCEPTIONS

So far we have looked at the consensual influence of television: at influences that varied from time to time but affected all or most citizens at any one time. Now we turn to non-consensual influences, differentiated influences, factors that affected some individuals but not others, or that affected different individuals in different ways. Such factors include their own personal characteristics, their social and political background, which newspapers they read, how much television news they watched, whether they watched television news on a particular day, and even whether they watched BBC or ITV on a particular day. We can use multiple regression analysis to discover the relative influence of these factors on perceptions. For consistency, we use a standard predictive scheme based upon thirty-five predictors representing the influences set out in the general model of media influence described in Chapter 1. These are:

1. Whether the individual identified with the Conservative Party, Labour, or the Alliance in the Pre-Campaign Wave.
2. Whether they claimed to be left-wing, right-wing, or neither at that time.
3. Their age, education, and strength of partisanship at that time.
4. Their interest in politics at four different times: the mid-term (early summer 1986), the pre-campaign week (March 1987), and the first and second fortnights of the final campaign. The first of these measured generalized interest in politics, the others measured interest in politics at particular times.
5. Their levels of political discussion in the pre-campaign week, the first fortnight, and the second fortnight of the campaign.
6. Whether they were motivated to follow the campaign for reinforcement, vote-guidance, information, or excitement. Motivations were measured in the second fortnight of the campaign, but the question wording was not time-specific (see Chapter 2).
7. Whether they read a highbrow paper at each of four time points: the mid-term, the pre-campaign week, the first and second fortnights of the campaign.
8. Whether they read a right-wing paper at each of these four time-points.
9. The number of TV news programmes they watched regularly (asked in the Pre-Campaign Wave).
10. Whether they listened to Radio 4 news regularly (asked in the Pre-Campaign Wave).

11. Whether they watched BBC-TV news regularly (asked in the Pre-Campaign Wave), and whether they had watched BBC-TV news on the day or day before the interview (in the first and second fortnight of the campaign).
12. As (11) for ITV news. Note, however, that over three-quarters of those who watched ITV news at any time had also watched BBC-TV news on the same day; and over 90 per cent of those who watched ITV news regularly also watched BBC-TV news regularly. Approximately, therefore, ITV news viewers were a subset of BBC-TV news viewers, not an alternative audience. Watching ITV news meant, in practice, watching more TV news.

It is a long list, but the SPSSX stepwise procedure seldom selected more than a few predictors as having a significant influence upon perceptions. However, it is important to recall the full list, in order to emphasize the factors that did *not* influence perceptions.

Whether people noticed the publication of opinion polls, whether they noticed local and national politicians, whether they noticed campaign themes—these seem relatively pure perceptions. No doubt a few treated awareness as implied approval, but for most people that did not seem to be so.

Perceptions of opinion polls changed dramatically during the campaign. In the pre-campaign week only 56 per cent had seen a recent opinion poll but this rose to 72 per cent in the first fortnight of the campaign and 77 per cent in the second. What they saw also changed. At all times, almost everyone who had seen a poll noticed that the Conservatives were top, but perceptions of which party was in second place varied sharply. In the Pre-Campaign Wave a majority of those who had seen a poll thought the Alliance was second. The percentage who had seen Labour in second place rose from a mere 13 per cent in the Pre-Campaign Wave to 78 per cent in the first fortnight and 95 per cent in the second.

Who noticed the opinion polls? Awareness of opinion polls was most predictable in the Pre-Campaign Wave and became steadily less predictable as the election approached and awareness became more widespread. Before the campaign opened the key influence on poll awareness was generalized interest in politics, but as the campaign drew to an end media use became

TABLE 7.5. *Multiple Regression Analyses of Awareness of Opinion Polls*

Pre-Campaign Wave	First Fortnight Wave	Second Fortnight Wave
25 Interest (GEN)	24 Interest (GEN)	18 BBC-TV (SF)
15 Discussion (PRE)	14 Discussion (FF)	16 Interest (GEN)
13 BBC-TV (SF)	11 BBC-TV (FF)	15 Discussion (SF)
11 Age		
RSQ 18	13	11

Notes: Calculated by SPSSX stepwise regression using the full set of predictors described in the text. Only those with a statistically significant influence are shown in the table.

Figures before the variable names are standardised regression coefficients ('path coefficients').

After each variable name is an indication of the time point at which it was measured.

It would simplify interpretation if the stepwise regression always selected predictors which were either general or contemporaneous, e.g. showing that BBC viewing in the first fortnight of the campaign influenced poll awareness at that time. However, we have not imposed that restriction on the regression programme and, occasionally, it selects a predictor measured later than the dependent variable. When that happens the contemporaneously measured predictor is usually almost (but not quite) as good a statistical predictor and the selection of a future-measured predictor should be treated as a statistical quirk. In fact, it is reassuring to find that even when strict time-sequence prediction is not imposed the regression usually finds that strict time-sequence provides the best statistical prediction. A great advantage of this open-minded approach is that it draws attention to the often contradictory influence of mid-term and campaign-time political interest. A narrower analytic strategy would have missed this important finding.

more important, especially viewing BBC-TV news (Table 7.5). These findings broadly echo those of Gunter, Svennevig, and Wober (1986, pp. 98–9), whose study of the 1983 election campaign showed that 'objectively measured knowledge was significantly correlated with *interest* in political discussion programmes both on radio and television, but with only one *news-consumption* variable—claimed viewing of television news' (italics added). In our analysis of the 1987 campaign we have distinguished more clearly between personal factors such as political interest and mobilizing factors such as television viewing; and we have detected a strong trend in the balance of influence between these two influences.

In the Pre-Campaign Wave there was a 41 per cent difference in awareness of polls between those with a high and low interest in politics. Following J. S. Coleman's terminology we can say that 'the effect of political interest on awareness of opinion polls was 41 per cent' in the Pre-Campaign Wave. But this effect had declined to only 22 per cent by the last fortnight of the campaign. Similarly, readers of lowbrow papers were relatively ill-informed about polls before the campaign but caught up on highbrow readers later: the effect of reading a highbrow paper declined from 33 per cent in the Pre-Campaign Wave to only 15 per cent in the closing stages of the campaign. By contrast, the difference between those who did and did not watch BBC-TV widened: so the effect of television viewing rose from 12 per cent in the Pre-Campaign Wave to 20 per cent in the last fortnight of the campaign. Thus, as the election approached, the basis of public awareness of opinion polls shifted from more personal factors like political interest or choice of paper, to more impersonal mobilizing factors like television news. The kinds of people who were most aware of public opinion polls in the closing stages of the campaign were very different from the kinds of people who were most aware of them in the mid-term (Table 7.6).

At the start of the campaign, constituency candidates were almost invisible to the electorate: very few electors claimed to have heard anything about them. Candidates became steadily more visible day by day throughout the campaign, however. Taking the first fortnight as a whole, four-fifths of voters had heard nothing about their local Conservative, Labour, and Alliance candidates but that figure dropped to little more than half in the second fortnight. So the election produced an enormous increase in at least minimal awareness of local candidates. Those who were more interested in politics and used more highbrow news sources tended to acquire more information about local candidates, and party supporters acquired more information about their own party's candidate, but none of these patterns was very strong or consistent. Information about local candidates was fairly haphazard.

TABLE 7.6. *Trends in Awareness of Opinion Polls*

	% who had seen recent poll		
	PRE	FF	SF
Amongst those who			
Had high interest in politics (GEN)	77	88	89
Had low interest in politics	36	51	67
Effect of high interest	41	37	22
Amongst those who			
Discussed politics often (CTP)	74	85	86
Discussed politics not at all	36	52	51
Effect of discussion	38	33	35
Amongst those who			
Read highbrow paper (GEN)	76	83	85
Read lowbrow paper	43	61	70
Effect of highbrow paper	33	22	15
Amongst those who			
Watched BBC TV news (CTP)	59	81	84
Did not	47	63	64
Effect of TV news	12	18	20

Notes: CTP = discussion and BBC-TV viewing measured 'contemporaneously', i.e. at same time as awareness of polls.
   High interest = 'a great deal' or 'quite a lot'.
   Low interest = 'not very much' or 'none at all'.
   For brevity, this table does not show trends amongst those with medium interest in politics, medium levels of political discussion, nor amongst those who read a middlebrow paper. The regressions shown in Table 7.5 include them, however.

We asked our panel whether they had, 'in the last few days, noticed anything in particular that Mrs Thatcher has said or done'; and similar questions about Kinnock, Steel, Owen, and 'other' (unspecified) Conservative, Labour, and Alliance leaders. By those measures of visibility, national politicians were much more visible than local candidates from the start. Indeed, Kinnock and Thatcher were more visible in our pre-campaign week, when both were on highly publicized foreign tours, than they

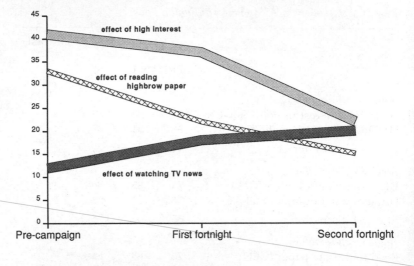

FIG. 7.4. Influences on Awareness of Polls (see Table 7.6)

were during the campaign itself. Their degree of visibility was also more predictable than the visibility of local candidates, though their visibility became less predictable as the election approached. Before the campaign opened those who were particularly interested in politics were very much more aware of Thatcher's and Kinnock's recent activities. By the end of the campaign that was no longer so true. Awareness of Thatcher and Kinnock was spread much more evenly throughout the electorate, and in so far as it did vary it was particularly high amongst those who had recently watched television news or had recently discussed the campaign (Table 7.7).

In the pre-campaign week, the effect of political interest on public awareness of Thatcher and Kinnock was 36 per cent and 45 per cent, respectively; but by the last fortnight of the campaign its effect had fallen to 17 per cent and 20 per cent respectively. The effect of reading a highbrow paper on public awareness of Kinnock dropped from 28 per cent to a mere 5 per cent as the election approached. Meanwhile, the effect of television viewing on public awareness of Thatcher's activities rose from 12 per cent to 20 per cent (Table 7.8). Such short-term 'closure of the knowledge gap' was noted by Blumler and McQuail (1968). Robinson (1972)

TABLE 7.7. *Multiple Regression Analyses of Thatcher's and Kinnock's Visibility*

Pre-Campaign Wave	First Fortnight Wave	Second Fortnight Wave
Thatcher's visibility		
29 Interest (GEN)	21 Discussion (PRE)	18 Discussion (SF)
−16 Lab ident (PRE)	15 Highbrow paper (SF)	15 BBC-TV (SF)
12 Discussion (PRE)	11 BBC-TV (SF)	11 ITV (FF)
−11 Excitement		
RSQ 16	9	8
Kinnock's visibility		
34 Interest (GEN)	14 Discussion (SF)	12 BBC-TV (SF)
13 Radio 4 (GEN)	14 Discussion (FF)	12 Discussion (SF)
		11 ITV (SF)
RSQ 15	6	6

Notes: See Table 7.5.

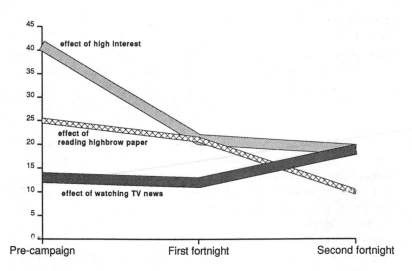

FIG. 7.5. Influences on Visibility of Thatcher and Kinnock (average) (see Table 7.8)

TABLE 7.8. *Trends in Thatcher's and Kinnock's Visibility*

	% who had noticed anything in particular done by					
	Thatcher			Kinnock		
	PRE	FF	SF	PRE	FF	SF
Amongst those who						
Had high interest in politics (GEN)	90	48	63	81	49	54
Had low interest in politics	54	23	46	36	33	34
Effect of interest	36	25	17	45	16	20
Amongst those who						
Discussed politics often (CTP)	89	53	63	74	57	52
Discussed politics not at all	59	21	27	45	18	23
Effect of discussion	30	32	36	29	39	29
Amongst those who						
Read highbrow paper (GEN)	91	54	57	78	58	45
Read lowbrow paper	69	30	43	50	41	40
Effect of highbrow paper	22	24	6	28	17	5
Amongst those who						
Watched BBC–TV news (CTP)	77	42	58	64	48	53
Did not	65	31	38	50	35	36
Effect of TV news	12	11	20	14	13	17

Notes: See Table 7.6.

found that, in America, the 'knowledge gap' was greater amongst those who relied on the press and smaller amongst those who relied upon television. So there are precedents for both our finding that knowledge spread through the electorate as the election approached and that television played a particular role in that process.

Somewhat in contrast to these findings about Thatcher and Kinnock, the visibility of all 'other' Conservative and Labour politicians (taken in each case as a collective, unspecified 'other') became *more* predictable as the election approached. With second-rank politicians, interest in politics continued to be a strong

TABLE 7.9. *Multiple Regression Analyses of 'Other' Conservative and Labour Politicians' Visibility*

Pre-Campaign Wave	First Fortnight Wave	Second Fortnight Wave
18 Interest (GEN)	15 Discussion (FF)	17 BBC-TV (SF)
18 Discussion (PRE)	13 Highbrow paper (GEN)	16 Discussion (PRE)
10 Age	13 BBC-TV (FF)	15 Interest (GEN)
10 Highbrow paper (SF)	12 Interest (GEN)	13 ITV (SF)
		10 Highbrow paper (SF)
RSQ 13	12	17

Notes: See Table 7.5.

predictor of their visibility, although the impact of television viewing also increased (Table 7.9).

Indeed, instead of declining, the effect of political interest on awareness of 'other' Conservative politicians actually rose from 32 per cent to 37 per cent between the Pre-Campaign Wave and the end of the campaign, and its effect on awareness of 'other' Labour politicians declined only from 38 per cent to 34 per cent. Overall, there remained a roughly constant difference between the interested and the uninterested. At the same time the effect of television viewing on public awareness of 'other' Conservatives rose from 11 per cent to 25 per cent while its effect on public awareness of 'other' Labour politicians rose from 6 per cent to 18 per cent (Table 7.10).

The influence of television on second-rank politicians' visibility is confirmed by a more detailed trend analysis. When people said they had noticed a Labour or Conservative politician other than Thatcher or Kinnock we asked them who had caught their attention. Denis Healey was noticed by 24 per cent in the Pre-Campaign Wave when he accompanied Kinnock on his visit to President Reagan. During the campaign itself Healey was noticed by only about 12 per cent on average but that concealed some sharp variations: 28 per cent noticed him in the last two days of the campaign, immediately after a spectacular on-screen row with *TV-am* presenter Ann Diamond.

Throughout the campaign we asked what people thought were the main issues being stressed by each of the parties. There were dramatic trends in public perceptions of, for example, the

Conservative Party's emphasis on defence. We have already related those trends to the content of television news. During the Pre-Campaign Wave, visits by Thatcher to Moscow and Kinnock to Washington naturally led to intense television coverage of defence issues. At that time both parties were clearly giving top priority to defence. When the campaign opened, it was not immediately obvious which particular issues the parties would choose to stress; but by the middle of the campaign it was clear that the Conservatives were focusing on defence issues where

TABLE 7.10. *Trends in 'Other' Politicians' Visibility*

| | % who have noticed anything in particular about | | | | | |
| | Other Conservatives | | | Other Labour | | |
	PRE	FF	SF	PRE	FF	SF
Amongst those who						
Had high interest in politics						
(GEN)	55	68	81	54	59	66
Had low interest in politics	23	37	44	16	24	32
Effect of interest	32	31	37	38	35	34
Amongst those who						
Discussed politics often (CTP)	53	70	74	46	57	62
Discussed politics not at all	18	27	41	19	18	19
Effect of discussion	35	43	33	27	39	43
Amongst those who						
Read highbrow paper (GEN)	50	73	76	50	56	63
Read lowbrow paper	21	39	53	21	28	30
Effect of highbrow paper	29	34	23	29	28	33
Amongst those who						
Watched BBC–TV news (CTP)	37	64	74	35	48	55
Did not	26	43	49	29	30	37
Effect of TV news	11	21	25	6	18	18

Notes: See Table 7.6.

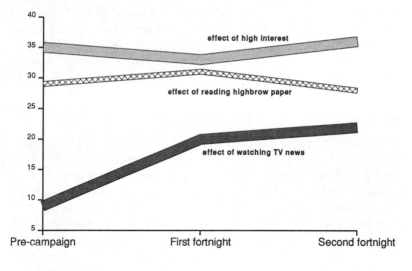

FIG. 7.6. Influences on Visibility of Other Politicians (average)
(see Table 7.10)

their policy was so much more popular than Labour's, if only
because it seemed so much simpler to explain. The public perceived enormous Conservative stress on defence in the Pre-
Campaign Wave and again in the latter half of the campaign, but
much less in the first half of the campaign.

None the less, despite these general trends in perceptions
there were always some voters who felt the Conservatives were
not stressing defence, just as there were always others who felt
the Conservatives were stressing defence. Those who were particularly interested in politics or discussed politics, read highbrow
papers or watched television news, were a little more likely to be
able to name some issues (*any* issues!) as the main themes being
stressed by the parties, but the level of predictability was low.

When it came to selecting particular issues, it was difficult to
predict who would name a particular issue. Depending upon the
date of the interview we could predict quite well whether people
would name defence as the Conservatives' main campaign theme,
but it was the date of the interview rather than the personal
characteristics of the interviewee that mattered. By the end of the
campaign, political interest, watching BBC-TV news, and a Labour

identity made people somewhat more inclined to name defence as the Conservative Party's main theme, however; and those who had frequent discussions about politics developed a particularly clear perception of the Conservatives' focus on defence issues (Table 7.11).

THE INFLUENCE OF PARTISANSHIP ON PERCEPTIONS

Perceptions of party chances were obviously influenced by opinion poll findings. Perceptions of Britain's economic performance and prospects were obviously influenced by objective economic factors and by government manipulation of economic statistics. None the less there remained deep personal prejudices that affected perceptions of both. Wishful thinking made political partisans more optimistic about their own party's prospects and more inclined to forecast their opponents' defeat. It made government supporters more optimistic about the economy and opposition supporters more pessimistic.

Opinion polls are more or less inaccurate measures of voting intentions. A succession of published polls typically produces a stream of more or less contradictory results. In part that may reflect real changes in public opinion but to a large extent it merely reflects sampling and other administrative errors. So if perceptions of party chances vary sharply with a succession of contradictory polls, it indicates that these perceptions are influenced by the published figures rather than by actual political preferences. People probably realize that their own circle of acquaintances is too narrow to provide a reasonable basis for estimating party chances and so they must rely on a combination of personal contacts, media comments, and especially published opinion polls. We have already noted the correlation between overall trends in perceptions of opinion polls and trends in perceptions of party prospects (see Table 7.3).

At any one time there were wide differences of opinion about party chances however. Some of those differences were relatively unpredictable. It was always fairly difficult to predict differences of opinion about Conservative and Alliance chances. In the pre-campaign week, Conservative voters were more optimistic about Conservative chances, Labour voters about Labour chances, and Alliance voters about Alliance chances; but the partisan influence

TABLE 7.11. *Trends in Public Perceptions of Conservative Party's Emphasis on Defence*

	% saying defence was Conservatives' main theme		
	PRE	FF	SF
Amongst those who			
Had high interest in politics (GEN)	45	18	57
Had low interest in politics	31	10	40
Effect of interest	14	8	17
Amongst those who			
Discussed politics often (CTP)	43	20	54
Discussed politics not at all	36	14	27
Effect of discussion	7	6	27
Amongst those who			
Read highbrow paper (GEN)	37	22	58
Read lowbrow paper	40	14	48
Effect of highbrow paper	−3	8	10
Amongst those who			
Watched BBC-TV news (CTP)	42	19	55
Did not	30	15	38
Effect of TV news	12	4	17
Amongst those who			
Listened to BBC Radio 4	47	21	52
Did not	39	16	48
Effect of listening to BBC Radio 4	8	5	4
Amongst those who			
Were Con identifiers (PRE)	40	20	43
Were Lab identifiers (PRE)	40	15	57
Were Alln identifiers (PRE)	43	14	46
Effect of being a Lab rather than Con identifier	0	−5	14

Notes: See Table 7.6. Party 'identifiers' include 'supporters' and 'leaners'.

on perceptions of Conservative and Alliance chances was much smaller than on perceptions of Labour chances. As the election approached, perceptions about party chances became more homogeneous and the predictability of different perceptions of Conservative and Alliance chances sank to a very low level: most voters thought that the Conservatives' chances were good and that Alliance chances were poor. Only a small and fairly random subset of voters disagreed.

Perceptions of Labour chances remained more predictable, though they also became rather more homogeneous as the campaign came to an end. On the evidence of our multiple regression analysis, partisanship exerted a consistently powerful influence on perceptions of Labour chances and by the end of the campaign it was the only remaining significant influence. In the pre-campaign week, other influences were also detectable: those who followed the campaign for excitement rated Labour chances highly; those who read right-wing papers or were themselves right-wing, those who watched BBC-TV news, and those who discussed politics a lot did not rate Labour chances highly.

Some of these influences carried forward into the first fortnight of the campaign, though they faded towards the end. There seem to be three broad influences at work here: a partisan influence, which was the most powerful and consistent, plus information-based and propaganda-based influences, which declined as the election approached. By the time of the election, even those with poor or biased information sources had enough accurate information to form the same judgement as those with better information sources. Only their own personal prejudices remained to influence their perceptions in one direction or another (Table 7.12).

Labour partisans were consistently very much more optimistic than Conservatives about the Labour Party's chances of victory; Alliance partisans had intermediate views on Labour chances, though they were inclined to the Conservative viewpoint in the Pre-Campaign Wave, but slightly more inclined to the Labour viewpoint by the end of the campaign. It is hardly surprising that political partisans claimed (at least) to be optimistic about their party's chances. But the trend analyses also confirm that press partisanship had a smaller but clear influence on perceptions amongst both Labour and Conservative identifiers. By the end of

TABLE 7.12. *Multiple Regression Analyses of Perceptions of Labour Chances*

Pre-Campaign Wave	First Fortnight Wave	Second Fortnight Wave
31 Lab ident	32 Lab ident	21 Lab ident
−12 Discussion (GEN)	−15 Rt paper (GEN)	−21 Con ident
−12 Rt paper (SF)	−11 Education (GEN)	
12 Excitement (GEN)		
−12 BBC-TV (FF)		
−10 On right		
RSQ 24	17	14

Notes: Express, Mail, Sun, Star, Telegraph, The Times coded 1 for right-wing; *Mirror, Guardian* coded 0 for left-wing; no paper coded 0.5 for intermediate.

See Table 7.5.

the campaign, Labour identifiers were 41 per cent more optimistic than Conservative supporters about Labour's chances. At the same time, Labour identifiers who read right-wing papers were 10 per cent less optimistic than Labour identifiers who did not; while Conservatives who read right-wing papers were similarly less optimistic about Labour's chances than Conservatives who did not read right-wing papers (Table 7.13).

Long-term trends suggest that economic optimism was highly volatile. It peaked in the election years of 1983 and 1987 and even the collapse of optimism over the period 1978–80 was halted and temporarily reversed at the 1979 election (*The Economist*, 1990, p. 34). Our own surveys confirm a strong switch towards optimism between our Mid-Term Wave in 1986 and our Pre-Campaign Wave in March 1987, but over the relatively short period from our Pre-Campaign Wave to the end of the campaign overall trends in economic perceptions were small. We asked our panel about their perceptions of the past year and the next year, about the economic trends affecting the country and the economic trends affecting their family. On balance the electorate was, and remained, strongly optimistic about the future for Britain and their family, strongly optimistic about Britain's performance in the past year, and optimistic (but much less so) about their own family's circumstances over the past year.

TABLE 7.13. *Trends in Perceptions of Labour Chances*

	% who think Labour has at least 'some' chance of a parliamentary majority		
	PRE	FF	SF
Amongst			
Lab identifiers (PRE)	62 (67)	73 (75)	81 (87)
Con identifiers (PRE)	21 (18)	34 (34)	43 (41)
Alln identifiers (PRE)	29 (28)	43 (46)	63 (59)
Effect of being a Con rather than Lab identifier	−41	−39	−38
Amongst Lab identifiers (PRE) who			
– read right-wing paper	54	73	73
– did not	64	73	83
Effect of right-wing paper on Lab identifiers	−10	0	−10
Amongst Con identifiers (PRE) who			
— read right-wing paper	16	27	39
— did not	27	44	48
Effect of right-wing paper on Con identifiers	−11	−17	−9

Note: Party 'identifiers' include 'supporters' and 'leaners'. Figures in brackets are for party 'supporters' only.

Our survey showed that there were strong partisan influences on switches in economic perceptions over the winter of 1986–7 (see Miller *et al.*, 1990, ch. 4) and partisan influences continued to influence the development of economic perceptions during the campaign itself. Economic perceptions were fairly predictable in the Pre-Campaign Wave and became more so towards the end of the campaign.

Partisan influences were strong and became stronger as the election approached. Perceptions of Britain's economic perform-ance were more predictable than those of family circumstances; and perceptions of the past were more predictable than expecta-tions for the future. Age influenced perceptions of family cir-

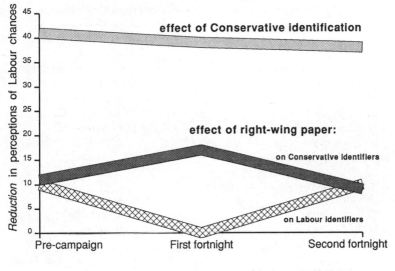

FIG. 7.7. Influences on Perceptions of Labour's Chances
(see Table 7.13)

cumstances (the older were more pessimistic than the young) but not perceptions of Britain's performance. Conversely, reading a right-wing paper had much more influence upon perceptions of Britain's performance than on perceptions of family circumstances. Remarkably, variables such as education and political discussion had relatively little influence on economic perceptions. The better educated were slightly more optimistic about the past (not the future, though) in the pre-campaign week but even this slight effect disappeared during the campaign. So, apart from age making people personally pessimistic about their own circumstances, economic perceptions were primarily influenced by a combination of personal political prejudice (partisanship) and biased information sources (right-wing or left-wing papers) (Table 7.14).

A trend analysis confirms these regression findings. There was always an enormous difference between the economic perceptions of those who initially had Conservative and Labour preferences, especially those who described themselves as party 'supporters'. The difference was largest when their focus was on Britain (not themselves) last year (not next year). Irrespective of the focus,

TABLE 7.14. *Multiple Regression Analyses of Economic Optimism*

Pre-Campaign Wave	Second Fortnight Wave
About British economy last year	
27 Con ident	29 Con ident
−21 Lab ident	−28 Lab ident
15 Rt paper (FF)	19 Rt paper (MID)
14 Education	10 Discussion (SF)
10 Discussion (PRE)	
RSQ 29	37
About British economy next year	
27 Con ident	29 Con ident
−17 Lab ident	19 Rt paper (PRE)
11 Rt paper (FF)	−13 Lab ident
RSQ 20	23
About family last year	
29 Con ident	−43 Lab ident
−14 Age	−19 Alln ident
13 Education	−14 Age
11 BBC-TV (FF)	
RSQ 14	17
About family next year	
32 Con ident	−31 Lab ident
−14 Age	−16 Age
12 Alln ident	−12 Alln ident
	12 Rt paper
RSQ 9	14

Notes: These questions were not asked in the First Fortnight Wave.
See notes to Table 7.12.

however, the difference widened as the election approached.
Because a majority of Conservative supporters were economic
optimists and a majority of Labour supporters were economic
pessimists, the difference between net optimism amongst Conservative and Labour supporters exceeded 100 per cent: it was
105 per cent in the Pre-Campaign Wave, rising to 121 per cent by
the end of the campaign. Amongst party identifiers as a whole,

the difference between Conservative and Labour optimism rose from 93 per cent in the Pre-Campaign Wave to 108 per cent by the end of the campaign.

Compared to this enormous influence of personal prejudice the influence of the media on economic perceptions was small but none the less significant. Amongst Labour partisans in particular the influence of the media more than doubled towards the end of the campaign, as Labour readers of right-wing papers switched from pessimism to optimism. The effect of reading a right-wing paper was to make Labour identifiers 12 per cent more optimistic in the Pre-Campaign Wave, and fully 30 per cent more optimistic by the end of the campaign (Table 7.15).

TABLE 7.15. *Trends in Economic Perceptions about British Economy Last Year by Partisanship and News Sources*

	% optimists *minus* % pessimists	
	PRE	SF
Amongst		
Conservative identifiers	79 (83)	93 (97)
Labour identifiers	−14(−22)	−15(−24)
Effect of being a Con rather than Lab identifier	93	108
Amongst Conservative identifiers (PRE) who		
— read right-wing paper	84	97
— did not	72	88
Effect of right-wing paper on Con identifiers	12	9
Amongst Labour identifiers (PRE) who		
— read right-wing paper	−5	9
— did not	−17	−21
Effect of right-wing paper on Lab identifiers	12	30

Note: Party 'identifiers' include 'supporters' and 'leaners'. Figures in brackets are for party 'supporters' only.

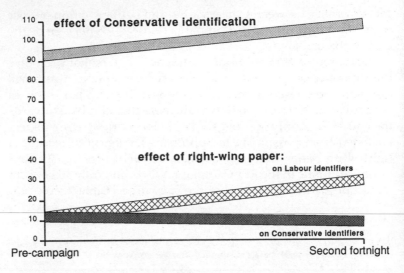

Fig. 7.8. Influences on Economic Optimism (see Table 7.15)

CONCLUSIONS

There can be no simple answer to the apparently simple question 'Does the media influence voters?' We need to distinguish between different elements of the media, and between the media's ability to inform and its ability to persuade. In this chapter we have looked at influences on public perceptions of politics, not at influences upon attitudes. From what we already knew about its audiences and programme content, we expected that television would have a stronger influence on public information and perceptions than on public attitudes and choices; while the press, particularly the mass-selling tabloids, would have a stronger influence on public attitudes and choices than on public information and perceptions.

Television news was pervasive, undifferentiated, and relatively unbiased. It proved immensely effective at communicating party campaign themes to the electorate, but in the short span of an election campaign it had only a small influence on the public's issue-agenda. The ebb and flow of controversy in television news items did not produce corresponding trends in public

interest and discussion. Television's failure to publicize the
unemployment issue was matched by only a small decline in
public concern about the issue while enormous public interest in
health, education and social services preceded television's switch
towards those issues. The most obvious test of television's
ability to set the public agenda was provided by its massive shift
of emphasis on to defence in the third week of the campaign.
That was matched by a similarly dramatic increase in public
perceptions that the party debate had now focused on defence,
but by only a small increase in the public's own concern about
the issue. While small influences in the short term may add up to
large influences in the longer term we must conclude that, within
an election campaign, television could influence but not dictate
the public agenda. However, it could dictate public perceptions
of the parties' agenda.

Television coverage had surprisingly little impact on trends in
party credibility. Public perceptions that the election was increasingly a two-horse race matched trends in published opinion
polls but preceded television's switch towards marginalizing the
Alliance by focusing on two-party controversy. Except in so far
as they publicized opinion poll findings, television projections
of party credibility did not dictate public perceptions.

In contrast to television, the press was highly differentiated:
different papers reached very different audiences with very
different messages. While the pervasiveness and uniformity of
television news made it unlikely that it would influence different
people in different ways, the press seemed likely to influence
different readers in very different ways. Since political bias was
so much a characteristic of the press we might expect its influence
to be more apparent in terms of attitudes than perceptions,
however. We looked at variations in perceptions across the
electorate to see whether television, the press, or both had any
influence. In general, the less objective the perception and the
more it was influenced by partisan factors, the greater the influence
of the press and the less the influence of television.

Public awareness of opinion polls was most predictable in the
Pre-Campaign Wave and became steadily less predictable as
the election approached and awareness spread throughout the
electorate. Before the campaign opened the key influence on poll
awareness was a generalized interest in politics, but as the

campaign drew to an end television viewing became more important. Before the campaign there was a 41 per cent difference in awareness of polls between those with high and low levels of interest in politics; but this declined to 22 per cent by the end of the campaign. Readers of lowbrow papers were relatively ill informed about polls before the campaign but caught up with highbrow readers later. Conversely the difference between those who did and did not watch television widened. As the election approached, the basis of awareness shifted from more personal resources like political interest or choice of paper, to more impersonal mobilizing factors like television news. The kinds of people who were aware of public opinion polls in the closing stages of the campaign were very different from the kinds of people who followed them in the mid-term.

Before the campaign opened those with a strong interest in politics were very much more aware of Thatcher's and Kinnock's recent activities. By the end of the campaign that was no longer so true: awareness of Thatcher and Kinnock had spread much more evenly through the electorate and in so far as it did vary it was particularly high amongst those who had recently watched television news or discussed the campaign. The difference between Kinnock's visibility to those with high and low levels of political interest dropped from 45 per cent before the campaign to 20 per cent at the end of the campaign; the difference between his visibility to highbrow and lowbrow paper readers dropped from 28 per cent to a mere 5 per cent; but over the same period the difference between his visibility amongst viewers and non-viewers of television news actually rose slightly. Once again this shows a switch from personal resources to media mobilization.

Somewhat in contrast to these findings about Thatcher and Kinnock, the visibility of all 'other' Conservative and Labour politicians, taken in each case as a collective 'other', became more predictable as the election approached. With these second-rank politicians, interest in politics continued to be a strong predictor of their visibility although the impact of television viewing also increased.

Those who were interested in politics or discussed politics, read highbrow papers or watched television news, were a little more likely to be able to name some issues as the main themes being stressed by the parties. When it came to naming particular issues, however, it was difficult to predict who would name which issue. Whether people named defence as the Conservatives' main campaign theme depended a great deal upon the date of the interview and rather less upon their personal characteristics or even their pattern of media use. This was a clear case of television influencing the electorate as a whole. None the less those who engaged in frequent political discussions became particularly aware of the Conservative Party's stress on defence.

We also looked at some perceptions which had attitudinal overtones. The conceptual distinction between perceptions and attitudes is clear; but perceptions of party chances or the state of the economy imply an element of approval or disapproval when articulated by the electorate. (They are purely objective perceptions · when articulated by political scientists or professional economists, of course.) These perceptions were influenced in varying degrees, though not completely determined, by partisan loyalties. As the election approached, perceptions about party chances of victory became more homogeneous: most voters thought Conservative chances were good and Alliance chances were poor. Perceptions of Labour chances remained more predictable, though they too became rather more homogeneous as the campaign came to an end. There were three broad influences on perceptions of Labour chances: a 'wishful thinking' (partisan) influence, which was the most powerful and consistent (Labour supporters rated their party's chances highly); a pure information-based influence (discussion, education, television viewing all lowered expectations of a Labour victory), which declined as the election approached; and a propaganda-based influence (reading right-wing papers also lowered expectations of a Labour victory), which also declined as the election approached. By the time of the election, even those with poor or biased information sources had enough accurate information to form the same judgement as those with better information sources. Only their own personal prejudices remained to influence their perceptions in one direction or another.

Economic perceptions were also influenced, very strongly, by partisanship, especially when the focus was on Britain (not the voters themselves) and on the preceding year (not the forthcoming year. Irrespective of the focus, however partisan influences on economic perceptions increased as the election approached.

Compared to the influence of personal partisan prejudice the influence of the media on economic perceptions was small but it also increased towards the end of the campaign, especially amongst Labour readers of right-wing papers.

8

Media Influence on Political Attitudes and Votes

PARTY AND LEADER IMAGES

Images of parties and party leaders are at the margin between perceptions and attitudes. We asked our panel to rate each of the parties on four scales: being united, having convincing policies, being likely to keep their promises, and being moderate. All of these images have overtones of approval as well as objective, factual perception. Similarly we asked the panel to rate the four party leaders, Thatcher, Kinnock, Steel, and Owen, on twelve more personal scales: being decisive, trustworthy, energetic, willing to listen, well informed, caring, a good leader of a team, tough, likeable, and standing up for Britain's interests against the European Community, the USA, and the USSR. Ratings consisted of 'marks out of ten' for how well the image label applied.

Factor analysis of these images indicated just one general factor underlying image scores for Kinnock, Steel, and Owen, but two general factors underlying scores for Thatcher. One grouped her images on being trustworthy, caring, likeable, and willing to listen, while the second grouped her images on being energetic, decisive, well informed, and tough. But irrespective of whether there was one general factor or two, it was clear that these general factors only explained a part of the variation in images of parties and leaders. Each of the individual images had a substantial component of uniqueness. We investigated both the common and the unique elements of these various images. For an overview we took each party's average score across the four party images, and each leader's average score across the twelve leader images. That approximated a factor analysis and is conceptually easier to explain. We also multiplied average scores by ten to eliminate decimal points, and turn them into percentages.

In the pre-campaign week, average Conservative and Alliance images were 10 per cent higher than Labour's but the gap was halved by the second fortnight of the campaign. Thatcher scored 8 per cent higher than the other leaders in the Pre-Campaign Wave, but by the end of the campaign all four leaders enjoyed very similar scores. Kinnock improved his score most, while Thatcher's actually declined.

Labour's rating on being united increased by 14 per cent though other aspects of its image improved by very much smaller amounts. Kinnock improved his image most on being energetic and decisive but actually lost ground on being able to stand up to the USSR, reflecting perhaps the consequences of his 'dad's army' interview with David Frost. Thatcher strengthened her image on being decisive but lost ground on being energetic.

At any one time, it was relatively easy to predict which electors would give parties and leaders high ratings. Ratings for the Conservative Party and for Thatcher were the most predictable, ratings for the Alliance and its leaders the least predictable. In addition, ratings for the two main parties and their leaders became more predictable as the election approached while those for the Alliance and its leaders became less predictable. In other words, perceptions of the Labour and Conservative Parties and their leaders became more polarized as the election approached, while perceptions of the Alliance and its leaders became more homogeneous. Thus by the last fortnight of the campaign, our regressions explained 59 per cent of the variation in Thatcher images but only 11 per cent of the variation in Alliance images (Tables 8.1, 8.2, 8.3).

As we might expect, partisanship was a major influence upon image ratings. Indeed it was *the* major influence on Conservative and Labour, Thatcher and Kinnock, and even Alliance images. But surprisingly perhaps, it was not the major influence on David Steel's image; and David Owen's image was influenced more by Labour partisanship than by Alliance partisanship: the hostility of Labour partisans towards Owen exceeded even the affection of Alliance partisans for him (Table 8.3).

Much less obviously, age proved a significant predictor of party and leader images. It was *the* main influence on Steel's image and a major influence on most other images, especially those of Owen and the Alliance but also those of Kinnock and

TABLE 8.1. *Multiple Regression Analyses of Conservative Party Image Ratings*

Pre-Campaign Wave	First Fortnight Wave	Second Fortnight Wave
Conservative Party image:		
61 Con ident	42 Con ident	42 Con ident
15 Alln ident	17 Rt paper (GEN)	20 Rt paper (Gen)
14 On right	−14 Lab ident	−16 Lab ident
−13 Education	14 Interest (PRE)	12 Age
12 Interest (GEN)	−11 On left	−11 On left
12 Interest (PRE)	8 Age	9 Interest (PRE)
9 Age		−8 Radio 4 (GEN)
9 BBC-TV (SF)		8 BBC-TV (SF)
−9 Discussion (FF)		
RSQ 47	48	55
Thatcher image		
40 Con ident	41 Con ident	41 Con ident
22 Age	−22 Lab ident	21 Rt paper (GEN)
−18 Lab ident	16 Age	20 Age
14 Interest (PRE)	16 Rt paper (GEN)	−17 Lab ident
12 Rt paper (FF)	12 Interest (PRE)	13 Interest (PRE)
8 Guidance	8 Information	−9 Interest (MID)
	−8 Education	8 Information
		8 BBC-TV (SF)
		−8 On left
RSQ 45	51	59

Notes: See Tables 7.5 and 7.12.

Thatcher. Older people were much more likely to give high ratings to politicians of all kinds and, to a lesser extent, to parties of all kinds.

Finally, media use had widespread effects. Reading a right-wing rather than a left-wing paper improved images of Thatcher and the Conservative Party, and damaged images of Kinnock and the Labour Party, though it had little or no influence on images of the Alliance and its leaders. Watching television had a much smaller effect and, like age, it had a positive effect upon images of all the parties and all the leaders.

Regression analyses suggest the influence of the press increased towards the end of the campaign. Trend analyses confirm the overwhelming impact of partisanship and the small, but increasing impact of the press. Thatcher's image ratings were 25 per cent higher amongst Conservative identifiers than amongst Labour identifiers in the Pre-Campaign Wave and became 30 per cent higher by the end of the campaign. Kinnock's image rating was 15 per cent lower amongst Conservative identifiers in the Pre-Campaign Wave and 18 per cent lower by the end of the campaign (Table 8.4).

Reading a right-wing rather than a left-wing paper made Labour identifiers 6 per cent more favourable to Thatcher and 6 per cent less favourable to Kinnock by the end of the campaign though the effects were smaller before that. A right-wing paper made Alliance identifiers 3 per cent less favourable to Kinnock and 8 per cent more favourable to Thatcher by the end of the campaign, and once again there was some evidence of a trend.

TABLE 8.2. *Multiple Regression Analyses of Labour Image Ratings*

Pre-Campaign Wave	First Fortnight Wave	Second Fortnight Wave
Labour Party Image		
39 Lab ident	42 Lab ident	44 Lab ident
15 Decision	15 Information	−17 Rt paper (GEN)
−14 Education	13 Age	12 Decision
−14 Rt paper (SF)	−13 Rt paper (MID)	13 Interest (FF)
	12 Interest (FF)	−11 Education
	−11 Education	
RSQ 28	31	33
Kinnock image		
38 Lab ident	35 Lab ident	44 Lab ident
−17 Rt paper (MID)	−18 Rt paper (GEN)	−20 Rt paper (GEN)
16 Age	18 Age	16 Age
14 Information	14 Information	14 Information
	13 BBC-TV (FF)	13 BBC-TV (FF)
	10 Reinforcement	
RSQ 24	26	32

Notes: See Tables 7.5 and 7.12.

TABLE 8.3. *Multiple Regression Analyses of Alliance Image Ratings*

Pre-Campaign Wave	First Fortnight Wave	Second Fortnight Wave
Alliance party image		
32 Alln ident	21 Alln ident	24 Alln ident
19 Age	17 Age	15 Age
16 Interest (PRE)	12 Interest (PRE)	12 Information
12 Reinforcement	13 Reinforcement	11 BBC-TV (SF)
RSQ 18	11	11
Steel image		
27 Age	26 Age	25 Age
25 Alln ident	18 Alln ident	17 Alln ident
14 Interest (PRE)	14 BBC-TV (SF)	11 BBC-TV (SF)
−11 Rt paper (SF)		−11 Rt paper (GEN)
RSQ 17	13	12
Owen image		
25 Alln ident	−30 Lab ident	−34 Lab ident
24 Age	21 Age	21 Age
17 Interest	−18 Con ident	−17 Con ident
	13 Information	12 Information
	13 ITV (SF)	
	10 Highbrow paper (GEN)	
RSQ 16	15	13

Notes: See Tables 7.5 and 7.12.

Press effects on Conservative identifiers were smaller. Clearly party and leader images were dominated by personal partisan prejudice and that domination increased towards the end of the campaign. None the less, there is evidence that the press had a small influence (Table 8.5).

Each aspect of party and leader images varied in a different way, some more predictably than others. Opinion on certain aspects of party and leader images was more polarized, on others more homogeneous; and different aspects of images were subject to different influences.

Images of unity were less influenced by partisanship and media bias, and less predictable overall, than other aspects of

TABLE 8.4. *Trends in Image Ratings by Partisanship*

	Average rating (marks × ten)		
	PRE	FF	SF
Conservative party images			
Amongst those who were			
— Con identifiers (PRE)	76 (77)	78 (79)	79 (81)
— Lab identifiers (PRE)	50 (48)	49 (47)	47 (45)
Effect of being a Con rather than Lab identifier	26	29	32
Thatcher images			
Amongst those who were			
— Con identifiers (PRE)	82 (83)	81 (83)	81 (82)
— Lab identifiers (PRE)	57 (56)	53 (51)	51 (48)
Effect of being a Con rather than Lab identifier	25	28	30
Labour Party images			
Amongst those who were			
— Con identifiers (PRE)	47 (45)	51 (50)	51 (49)
— Lab identifiers (PRE)	64 (66)	69 (71)	71 (74)
Effect of being a Con rather than Lab identifier	−17	−18	−20
Kinnock images			
Amongst those who were			
— Con identifiers (PRE)	55 (54)	61 (60)	59 (58)
— Lab identifiers (PRE)	70 (72)	73 (75)	77 (79)
Effect of being a Con rather than Lab supporter	−15	−12	−18

Note: Party 'identifiers' include 'supporters' and 'leaners'. Figures in parentheses are for party 'supporters' only.

party images. Thatcher's image of being tough and decisive was the least predictable—not, of course, because these two labels seemed inappropriate but because there was such general agreement that they were appropriate. Few voters gave her low ratings for being tough or decisive, and they were an unpredictable few. In sharp contrast, opinion was more divided on whether she was

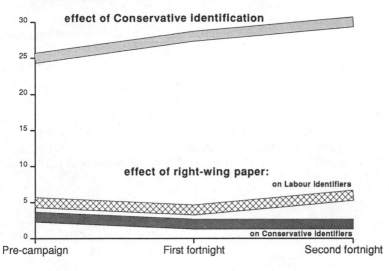

FIG. 8.1. Influences on Thatcher's Image (see Tables 8.4 and 8.5)

trustworthy, caring, or willing to listen: Conservatives were inclined to give her high marks on these matters while others were not.

Age was the main influence upon all politicians' ratings for being energetic. Older people were much more impressed by politicians' energy than were younger people. Partisanship took second place when it had an influence at all, and often it did not.

Press bias (that is, reading a right-wing or left-wing paper) had a relatively large influence upon Thatcher's image of being willing to listen, caring, and likeable. On all these 'softer' virtues, readers of right-wing papers gave Thatcher high marks, while readers of left-wing papers did not (even when we take account of people's own partisanship, as the regression analysis does automatically). Reading right-wing papers also made people more inclined to believe the Conservative Party had convincing policies and was likely to keep its promises, that Kinnock was neither decisive, nor trustworthy, nor a good leader of a team, and especially that he could not be relied upon to stand up for British interests against the USSR. Thus, reading right-wing papers had most effect upon increasing Thatcher's ratings on the 'soft' virtues and depressing Kinnock's ratings on the 'hard' virtues—that is, on those aspects of each politician's image where they were generally considered to be at their weakest. The press did not reverse general perceptions of party leaders: it sharpened and reinforced images they already had. A bad press highlighted what were generally agreed to be a politician's weak points; a good press encouraged people to give politicians even higher ratings on their generally acknowledged strengths.

Defence policy and relationships with the Soviet Union played an unusually large part in political debate in 1987. During our Pre-Campaign Wave Thatcher's visit to Moscow and Kinnock's

TABLE 8.5. *Trends in Image Ratings by Partisanship and News Sources*

	Average rating (marks × ten)		
	PRE	FF	SF
Thatcher image ratings			
Amongst Con identifiers (PRE) who			
— read right-wing papers	83	82	82
— did not	80	80	80
Effect of right-wing paper on Con identifiers	3	2	2
Amongst Lab identifiers (PRE) who			
— read right-wing papers	60	56	55
— did not	55	52	49
Effect of right-wing paper on Lab identifiers	5	4	6
Kinnock image ratings			
Amongst Con identifiers (PRE) who			
— read right-wing papers	53	58	56
— did not	59	64	63
Effect of right-wing paper on Con identifiers	−6	−6	−7
Amongst Lab identifiers (PRE) who			
— read right-wing papers	68	70	72
— did not	71	74	78
Effect of right-wing paper on Lab identifiers	−3	−4	−6

Note: Party 'identifiers' include 'supporters' and 'leaners'.

to Washington drew attention to the issue. In the final campaign, Conservative propaganda focused on defence and Kinnock himself provided a target for attack in a *TV-am* interview with David Frost in which, his opponents alleged, he advocated a strategy of guerrilla war as an alternative to nuclear weapons. On being able to stand up to the USSR, Thatcher scored 80 per cent in the pre-campaign week, easing to 79 per cent in the last fortnight of the campaign. Kinnock scored only 61 per cent in the pre-campaign week—the same as his average score across all image aspects. By the end of the campaign, his average image score had risen to 65 but his score on standing up to the USSR had dropped to 56. By the end of the campaign it was the weakest aspect of his image.

Scores on this image (standing up to the USSR) were never very predictable for any politician. Partisanship was the main influence on Thatcher's and Kinnock's scores but not Steel's or Owen's; and even for Thatcher and Kinnock the partisan influence was weaker than on other aspects of their image. Reading a right-wing paper never had any significant effect on this aspect of Thatcher's image and only a small effect on Kinnock's image in the Pre-Campaign Wave, though its influence grew steadily thereafter: in the first fortnight of the campaign press bias was a little more influential than anything except partisanship and in the second fortnight it was far more influential than anything except partisanship (Table 8.6).

As the campaign developed Kinnock's image as a man who would stand up to the USSR declined throughout the electorate, even amongst Labour supporters, though it declined slightly more amongst Conservative supporters. Amongst both Labour

TABLE 8.6. *Multiple Regression Analyses of Kinnock's Image for Standing up to the USSR*

Pre-Campaign Wave	First Fortnight Wave	Second Fortnight Wave
22 Lab ident	26 Lab ident	34 Lab ident
−16 Con ident	−19 Rt paper (GEN)	−24 Rt paper (GEN)
16 Guidance	−15 Education	15 Guidance
15 Age	14 Information	14 Age
−13 Rt paper (MID)		
RSQ 22	18	25

and Conservative identifiers, it declined twice as much if they read a right-wing paper. The decline was never great, but it has to be judged against the fact that his general image was improving sharply (Table 8.7).

TABLE 8.7. *Trends in Kinnock's Image Ratings for Standing up to the USSR*

	Average rating (marks × ten)		
	PRE	FF	SF
Amongst			
Con identifiers (PRE)	53 (52)	51 (49)	47 (45)
Lab identifiers (PRE)	72 (74)	67 (68)	69 (70)
Alln identifiers (PRE)	60 (61)	56 (56)	54 (54)
Effect of being a Con rather than Lab identifier	−19	−16	−22
Amongst Con identifiers (PRE) who			
— read right-wing paper	50	47	43
— did not	57	56	53
Effect of right-wing paper on Con identifiers	−7	−9	−10
Amongst Lab identifiers (PRE) who			
— read right-wing paper	70	66	63
— did not	73	68	71
Effect of right-wing paper on Lab identifiers	−3	−2	−8

Note: Party 'identifiers' include 'supporters' and 'leaners'. Figures in parentheses are for party 'supporters' only.

EXPLICIT ATTITUDES

Questions about perceptions were framed in terms of awareness rather than approval, though the partisan nature of the answers often betrayed a lack of objectivity. We found that television had a large effect on those political perceptions which had little or no attitudinal content. But on political perceptions where there were elements of approval or disapproval media effects were much smaller, and it was the press, rather than television, which had more impact.

We turn now to influences on attitudes and votes. Attitude questions explicitly sought statements of choice, preference, approval, or disapproval. Given our findings on perceptions we should expect the press to have more influence than television on attitudes. Whether its influence was large or small remains to be seen.

We sought to measure attitudes in several ways. We asked respondents to give each party a mark out of ten for its handling of four issues: unemployment, inflation, defence, and a composite 'health, education, and social services'. We also asked them to name the party they thought best on economic matters for themselves and their families, for Britain as a whole, and for the unemployed. We asked for thermometer ratings (out of 100) for how warm people felt towards parties and their leaders. After the election, we asked whether the parties should change their leaders, their policies, or both.

In addition, we asked about voting preferences. In the Pre-Campaign Wave and the two Campaign Waves we asked electors to give each party a mark out of ten for how inclined they were to vote for it. After the election we asked which way they had actually voted.

Total system approval

Where we asked for marks out of ten, or thermometer ratings out of a hundred, we can use relative scores for different parties to construct measures of preference. But we can also add the scores for all three parties (Conservative, Labour, Alliance) in order to get a measure of *total system approval*. One person might give the Conservative Party the highest of three high scores, another might give it the highest of three low scores. Both would thereby indicate a preference for the Conservative Party but their attitudes would not be the same. Not surprisingly, total system approval proved much less predictable than relative preference. None the less, variations in levels of total system approval were not entirely random.

The most powerful and consistent influence on total approval was political interest. Those who found the events of the campaign interesting very consistently recorded *higher* levels of total approval. At the same time there was some evidence that those who had a more general interest in politics, as distinct from those who found the campaign interesting (a distinction we have already found significant in other contexts), were likely to record *lower* levels of total approval.

Media influence was small but consistent. Despite complex controls for various aspects of political interest and for other influences, those who watched a lot of television news, especially on BBC-TV, showed higher levels of total approval. So did older people. Those with high levels of education were hard to please: they showed particularly low levels of total system approval. Conservatives and right-wingers were more satisfied with the parties, Labour identifiers and left-wingers less satisfied. All of these findings remained broadly similar irrespective of whether we analysed total warmth towards parties and party leaders, total ratings for the parties' performance on issues, or total inclinations towards voting for all three leading parties (Table 8.8).

Relative preference

Suppose someone gives marks C, L, and A to the Conservatives, Labour, and Alliance for their handling of the unemployment issue, where each of C, L, and A is a mark out of ten. Their measure of total approval for the parties on unemployment is thus (C+L+A). We can calculate their relative preference for the Conservatives on the unemployment issue as C/(C+L+A), that is, as the mark given to the Conservatives expressed as a proportion of the total mark given to all three parties (or multiplied by 100 to transform it from a proportion into a percentage). Regression analyses of such relative preferences show:

1. Relative preferences for the Alliance were much less predictable than for Labour or Conservative.
2. Relative preferences for Labour and Conservative tended to be inversely related.
3. Media influences on relative preferences for the Alliance were always weak and usually insignificant.
4. Media influences on relative preferences for Conservative and Labour were always significant, usually similar in magnitude but opposite in sign.

TABLE 8.8. *Multiple Regression Analyses of Total System Approval*

Pre-Campaign Wave	First Fortnight Wave	Second Fortnight Wave

Predicting total marks for Con plus Lab plus Alln handling of four issues

Pre-Campaign Wave	First Fortnight Wave	Second Fortnight Wave
28 Interest (PRE)	24 Interest (FF)	19 Interest (FF)
−15 Interest (GEN)	15 Age	17 Age
11 BBC-TV	14 Right/left	16 Con ident
	12 Num TV (GEN)	−16 Education
	11 Guidance	15 Guidance
		11 Discussion (PRE)
RSQ 8	15	18

Predicting total thermometer ratings for party leaders

Pre-Campaign Wave	First Fortnight Wave	Second Fortnight Wave
−16 Lab ident	−19 On left	−24 Interest (GEN)
15 On right	17 Interest (FF)	22 Con ident
13 Interest (PRE)	13 Con ident	15 Information
	10 Information	13 Interest (FF)
		13 BBC-TV (FF)
		11 Interest (SF)
		11 Discussion (PRE)
		11 Num TV (GEN)
RSQ 10	13	18

Predicting total thermometer ratings for three parties

Pre-Campaign Wave	First Fortnight Wave	Second Fortnight Wave
−19 Lab ident	20 Interest (FF)	−22 Interest (GEN)
13 Reinforcement	−14 On left	17 Con ident
12 Interest (PRE)	13 BBC-TV (GEN)	17 Interest (SF)
	11 Con ident	13 Interest (FF)
		11 BBC-TV (FF)
		11 Num TV (GEN)
RSQ 7	10	14

Predicting total marks for inclination to vote for three parties

Pre-Campaign Wave	First Fortnight Wave	Second Fortnight Wave
16 Num TV (GEN)	21 Interest (FF)	−19 Lab ident
14 Interest (FF)	16 Guidance	17 Interest (FF)
12 Guidance	−14 Discuss (SF)	16 Num TV (GEN)
11 On right	−12 Education	16 Guidance
10 Information		−15 Interest (GEN)
		13 Interest (SF)
		−12 Education
RSQ 11	10	20

Notes *over/*

Notes: Because of the potential significance of partisan and ideological influences on explicit attitudes and voting choice, we imposed particularly stringent controls for these variables in this and subsequent tables. This strengthens our conclusions about the impact of media partisanship, but it requires a variety of measures of partisanship and ideological backgrounds. We used as potential predictors all the variables used in previous regressions, which include party identification plus being 'On left' or 'On right'. We now add 'Right/left'. 'On left' contrasts self-described left-wingers with others; 'On right' similarly contrasts self-described right-wingers with others; but 'Right/left' is a spectrum, with centrists treated as intermediate between right-wingers and left-wingers. Using these three potential predictors in an SPSSX stepwise regression strategy gave us the greatest possible chance of detecting influences from the voter's own ideology. If, despite this, the ideology of the voter's newspaper is selected by the stepwise regression procedure (as it is in later tables, though not in Table 8.8), then we can be confident that we really are measuring the impact of the paper's ideology and not the impact of the voter's ideology.

When calculating the total thermometer ratings of party leaders, Steel's and Owen's ratings were averaged before adding their average to the ratings of Thatcher and Kinnock. That prevented the Alliance's dual leadership distorting the analysis.

See also notes to Tables 7.5 and 7.12.

So we can simplify the analysis of relative preferences by focusing on the electorate's relative preference for the Conservatives rather than Labour, that is on $(C-L)/(C+L+A)$.

Naturally, Conservative identifiers gave relatively high marks to the Conservative Party, Labour identifiers to Labour, and Alliance identifiers to the Alliance. Voters' ideological self-placement on a left–right scale also tended to predict their relative preferences for the Conservative or Labour Parties. It would be very surprising if partisanship and ideology did not affect relative preferences in this way, but it is essential to control for partisanship and ideology before investigating other, less obvious influences.

Even with stringent controls for partisanship and ideology, multiple regression analyses show that the press had a significant influence on preferences. Those who read right-wing papers proved significantly more satisfied with the Conservative Party's handling of major issues, even when we controlled for their party identification and ideological self-placement. Indeed, the ideological leanings of readers' papers had more impact than their own ideology. The press had a substantial influence on their choice of the best party on economic matters, both for themselves and for Britain as a whole; and, indeed, on their assessments of overall party performance across the full range of economic, defence, and social issues (Table 8.9).

TABLE 8.9. *Multiple Regression Analyses of Relative Assessments of Party Performance on Policy Issues*

Pre-Campaign Wave	First Fortnight Wave	Second Fortnight Wave
Predicting choice of best party on economic matters for citizens and their families		
75 Con ident	−64 Lab ident	−65 Lab ident
30 Alln ident	−28 Alln ident	−26 Alln ident
9 Rt paper (MID)	14 Rt paper (GEN)	15 Rt paper (GEN)
−9 ITV (GEN)	13 Highbrow paper (GEN)	11 Highbrow paper (GEN)
	−9 Strength ident	7 Education
RSQ 48	46	48
Predicting choice of best party on economic matters for Britain as a whole		
47 Con ident	−75 Lab ident	41 Con ident
−37 Lab ident	−32 Alln ident	−34 Lab ident
8 Rt paper (MID)	20 Rt paper (GEN)	16 Rt paper (GEN)
7 BBC-TV (GEN)	8 Num TV (GEN)	−8 On left
	−7 Strength ident	7 Highbrow paper (GEN)
RSQ 63	63	63
Predicting relative preferences on unemployment, inflation, defence and social issues (overall average preference)		
37 Con ident	36 Con ident	32 Con ident
−28 Lab ident	−22 Lab ident	−22 Lab ident
13 Rt paper (MID)	17 Rt paper (GEN)	22 Right/left
12 Right/left	14 Right/left	19 Rt paper (GEN)
9 Interest (GEN)	−9 Guidance	
RSQ 51	48	53

Note: See Table 8.8.

More detailed analysis suggests the press was more successful at influencing assessments of party performance on unemployment than on other issues. It had a particularly strong influence amongst Labour identifiers, especially towards the end of the campaign. Amongst Labour identifiers, the effect of reading a right-wing paper on their relative preference for the Conservatives on unemployment was 13 per cent in the Pre-Campaign Wave, rising to 19 per cent by the second half of the campaign (Table 8.10).

TABLE 8.10. *Trends in Assessments of Relative Party Performance on Handling Unemployment* (marks × 10)

	Con rating *minus* Lab rating		
	PRE	FF	SF
Amongst			
Con identifiers (PRE)	18	10	10
Lab identifiers (PRE)	−36	−39	−44
Effect of being a Con rather than Lab identifier	54	49	54
Amongst Con identifiers (PRE) who			
– read right-wing paper	20	13	12
— did not	16	7	7
Effect of right-wing paper on Con identifiers	4	6	5
Amongst Lab identifiers (PRE) who			
— read right-wing paper	−26	−27	−30
— did not	−39	−42	−49
Effect of right-wing paper on Lab identifiers	13	15	19

Note: Party 'identifiers' include 'supporters' and 'leaners'.

The press also had a moderately strong influence on public feelings of warmth towards parties and their leaders. Once again, the ideological leanings of readers' papers were more influential than their own ideological leanings, though less than their partisanship (Table 8.11) Once again, the press had a

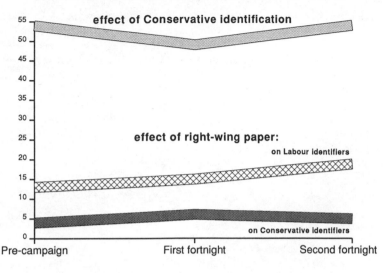

F I G. 8.2. Influences on Ratings of Parties on Unemployment
(see Table 8.10)

particularly strong influence on Labour identifiers; and its influence increased at the end of the campaign (Table 8.12).

Pre-campaign party identification exercised a particularly strong
influence on voting preferences throughout the campaign and
on final voting choices in the election itself. None the less, the
press still showed a moderately powerful influence on voting
even when we controlled for voters' initial partisanship and
ideology (Table 8.13) It had most effect upon those who were
initially undecided or were Alliance identifiers. Amongst those
who were Conservative or Labour before the campaign, press
bias had about a 6 per cent effect; amongst those who originally
had an Alliance preference it had a 23 per cent effect; while
amongst those who were originally undecided it had a 28 per
cent effect—measuring all these effects in terms of the Conservative lead over Labour (Table 8.14).

After the election we asked whether each of the parties should
now change its leaders, its policy, or both. Most voters agreed
that changes were needed in the Alliance and a large majority felt
changes (at least in policy) were also needed in the Labour Party,
but views were split almost exactly half-and-half on whether the

TABLE 8.11. *Multiple Regression Analyses of Relative Preferences on Party and Leader Thermometers*

Pre-Campaign Wave	First Fortnight Wave	Second Fortnight Wave
Predicting relative warmth towards parties		
−65 Lab ident	−31 Lab ident	36 Con ident
−27 Alln ident	30 Con ident	−34 Lab ident
15 Rt paper (MID)	20 Rt paper (GEN)	16 Rt paper (GEN)
13 Right/left	−18 On left	−10 On left
	8 ITV (GEN)	10 Rt paper (MID)
		−10 Interest (GEN)
		9 Highbrow paper (GEN)
RSQ 55	58	66
Predicting relative warmth towards leaders		
34 Con ident	−31 Lab ident	36 Con ident
−33 Lab ident	28 Con ident	−30 Lab ident
14 Rt paper (MID)	19 Rt paper (GEN)	20 Rt paper (GEN)
10 Right/left	18 Right/left	−15 On left
	8 ITV (GEN)	
RSQ 53	56	59

Notes: Using parties' and leaders' initials, relative warmth towards parties was defined as $(C-L)/(C+L+A)$; and relative warmth towards leaders as $(T-K)/(T+K+(S+O)/2)$.

See also notes to Table 8.8.

Conservatives should change anything after this, their third electoral victory. Naturally Conservative identifiers were least inclined to advocate changes in the Conservative Party, but so were readers of right-wing papers and, to a lesser extent, readers of highbrow papers (Table 8.15).

THE LONGER TERM

A year before their landslide victory in the election of June 1987 the Conservatives lagged behind Labour in the opinion polls. Most of the swing to the Conservatives between the summer of 1986 and the summer of 1987 occurred during the winter of 1986–7, and there was relatively little swing in the last few months before the election. What part did the media play in that year-long process? Since we do not have a year-long content analysis of the media we cannot investigate the influence of a changing media consensus but we can analyse the differential effects of different elements of the media. To what extent did persistently reading different papers or regularly watching different television channels make a difference to swings in political preferences?

For this longer-term analysis we have taken those panel members who were interviewed in the Mid-Term Wave (April–May 1986), the Pre-Campaign Wave (March–April 1987), and the Post-Election Wave (June 1987). We have restricted the analysis to the

TABLE 8.12. *Trends in Relative Warmth towards Thatcher and Kinnock* (100° thermometers)

	Warmth towards Thatcher *minus* warmth towards Kinnock		
	PRE	FF	SF
Amongst			
Con identifiers (PRE)	41	31	32
Lab identifiers (PRE)	−28	−36	−44
Effect of being a Con rather than Lab identifier	69	67	76
Amongst Con identifiers (PRE) who			
— read right-wing paper	42	34	35
— did not	39	27	27
Effect of right-wing paper on Con identifiers	3	7	8
Amongst Lab identifiers (PRE) who			
— read right-wing paper	−19	−29	−31
— did not	−32	−39	−49
Effect of right-wing paper on Lab identifiers	13	10	18

Note: Party 'identifiers' include 'supporters' and 'leaners'.

TABLE 8.13. *Multiple Regression Analyses of Relative Voting Preferences and Voting Choice*

Predicting voting preferences			Predicting vote
PRE	FF	SF	POST
−41 Lab ident	36 Con ident	−71 Lab ident	46 Con ident
37 Con ident	−35 Lab ident	31 Alln ident	−41 Lab ident
15 Rt paper	15 Right/left	23 Rt paper	14 Rt paper
(MID)	10 Rt paper	(GEN)	(GEN)
12 Right/left	(MID)	13 Highbrow	9 Discussion
	11 Highbrow	paper (GEN)	(SF)
	paper (MID)	−11 On left	
	9 Rt paper	−11 Interest	
	(GEN)	(GEN)	
RSQ 70	67	71	78

Notes: For simplicity, this table does not show a few influences that were statistically significant but had coefficients of less than 9.

Actual votes measured in Post-Election Wave.

772 people who were interviewed in all three waves. We have classified newspaper readers by their persistent choice of paper-type. We divide newspapers into six types:

1. no paper
2. the *Express* or the *Mail*
3. the *Mirror*
4. the *Sun* or the *Star*
5. the *Telegraph*, *The Times*, or the *Financial Times*
6. the *Guardian*

and classify voters as 'persistent' readers if they were 'regular' readers of the same paper-type in both the Mid-Term and Pre-Campaign Waves, that is, if they regularly read the same paper-type throughout the year preceding the election. No one suggests that occasional exposure to the *Sun* or *The Times* will have an instant effect upon political opinions. But persistent exposure to the same paper-type at least three times a week for a whole year may well have some effect, particularly if it is a pre-election year when the political temperature usually rises.

TABLE 8.14. *Conservative Lead over Labour in Votes* (%)

Amongst Con identifiers (PRE) who	
— read right-wing papers	90
— did not	83
Effect of right-wing paper on Con identifiers	7
Amongst Lab identifiers (PRE) who	
— read right-wing papers	−76
— did not	−81
Effect of right-wing paper on Lab identifiers	5
Amongst Alln identifiers (PRE) who	
— read right-wing papers	16
— did not	−7
Effect of right-wing paper on Alln identifiers	23
Amongst those with no party identification (PRE) who	
— read right-wing papers	33
— did not	5
Effect of right-wing paper on those with no party identification	28

Note: Actual votes measured in the Post-Election Wave.

With a small sample it is not advisable to carry out the analysis in terms of individual papers since so few respondents read *any* single paper. Grouping readers of roughly similar papers together improves the statistical reliability of our results. No matter how small the sample size, however, it would obscure the analysis to group readers of very different papers, such as the *Guardian* and the *Telegraph*, together. *Guardian* readers are sufficiently interesting and distinctive that it is worth tolerating the statistical uncertainties caused by our small sample and the *Guardian's* small readership. In classifying people as persistent readers, we have allowed them to switch between different individual papers, provided they stayed with the same paper-type. Once again this is to retain larger numbers in the analysis and maximize the statistical reliability of the conclusions.

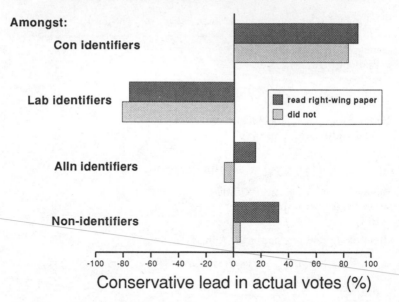

FIG. 8.3. Influence of Right-Wing Paper on Vote (see Table 8.14)

TABLE 8.15. *Multiple Regression Analyses of whether Parties should change their Leaders and/or Policies*

	Post-Election Wave
Conservative Party should change:	−35 Con ident −23 Rt paper (GEN) −14 Highbrow paper (GEN) RSQ 22
Labour Party should change:	−22 Lab ident −12 Excitement −11 Interest (GEN) RSQ 8
Alliance should change:	No significant patterns (almost universal assent!)

Not everyone proved to be a persistent reader of one paper (or even of a group of similar papers) but the majority did. Just over two-thirds fell into one of our six categories of persistent readers (or persistent non-readers). Some changed their paper-types, and others were persistent readers of a myriad of papers with individual readerships too small for us to analyse (the *Scotsman*, the *Glasgow Herald*, and regional English papers, for example).

Unfortunately our Mid-Term Wave was drawn from the 1986 British Social Attitudes Survey which asked no questions about television viewing or radio listening. So we have had to classify viewing and listening by respondents' reports of their 'regular' behaviour in March 1987. How long-term those viewing and listening habits were we cannot say. We have classified them in two ways. First, we have divided viewers into those who regularly watched BBC-TV news only, those who regularly watched ITV news only, and those who regularly watched *both* (negligible numbers of voters watched neither). Second, we have divided voters into those who regularly viewed or listened to any high-brow news programmes such as BBC-TV's *Newsnight*, ITV's *Channel 4 News*, or the BBC's Radio 4 news, and those who did not.

In the Mid-Term Wave, a year before the election, *Guardian* and *Mirror* readers were strongly Labour; *Express*, *Mail*, and *Telegraph* readers were strongly Conservative. Support for the Alliance was weaker amongst readers of the tabloids than readers of the quality press: all perhaps as expected. Rather more surprisingly perhaps, *Sun* and *Star* readers (taken together) were at that time split fairly evenly between Labour and Conservative with the Alliance a fairly close third.

Sun/Star readers were distinctive in other ways. They were not quite the least well educated: in our panel, *Mirror* readers had slightly less professional qualifications than even *Sun/Star* readers, though every other paper's readers (and non-readers) had much more. But *Sun/Star* readers were less interested in politics even than *Mirror* readers; and they were the least likely to tune in to highbrow news programmes such as *Newsnight*, *Channel 4 News*, or Radio 4 news. Most clearly of all, *Sun/Star* readers were uniquely uncommitted to party politics. In the mid-term, fully 70 per cent of *Mirror* readers not only had a party preference but regarded themselves as party 'supporters'. The corresponding

percentage of party 'supporters' amongst *Guardian* readers was
66 per cent, amongst *Telegraph* etc., readers 62 per cent, and
amongst *Express/Mail* readers 56 per cent. Amongst *Sun/Star*
readers it was a mere 41 per cent. So there was a sharp contrast
between relatively committed *Mirror* readers and relatively uncommitted *Sun/Star* readers despite their similarities in terms of
class and education.

It was a contrast with important implications for the future.
Over the following year *Mirror* readers as well as *Guardian* and
Telegraph readers proved relatively stable in their political preferences. On election day, in June 1987, 84 per cent of *Mirror*
readers (and only slightly less *Guardian* and *Telegraph/Times/*
Financial Times readers) voted for the party they had preferred a
year earlier, in the summer of 1986. But only 64 per cent of *Sun/*
Star readers did so. *Sun/Star* readers were more likely than others
to have no preference at all in 1986 (despite voting in 1987), and at
the same time, those *Sun/Star* readers who did have a preference
in 1986 were more likely than others to change it during the next
year (Table 8.16).

TABLE 8.16. *Profiles of Persistent Newspaper Readers* (%)

Persistently read (1986–7)	High educ. qual.	Highbrow TV or radio	Political interest	Party 'supporter' in 1986 mid-term	Constant party choice 1986–7
No paper	37	45	79	58	75
Express/Mail	22	37	80	56	78
Mirror	2	26	75	70	84
Sun/Star	11	18	55	41	64
Telegraph etc.	50	77	97	62	83
Guardian	65	72	96	66	82

Notes: *Telegraph* etc. = *Telegraph, The Times, Financial Times.*
  High educ. qual. = Had degree or professional qualification.
  Highbrow TV or radio = Regularly tuned in to BBC's *Newsnight,*
Channel 4 News, or Radio 4 news.
  Political Interest = Found what was happening in politics at least
'fairly' interesting (Pre-Campaign Wave).
  Constant party choice = Voted in 1987 for the party which they had
preferred in 1986.

Overall, in this panel, the Conservative lead over Labour increased by 10 per cent between 1986 and election day in 1987. It increased by 17 per cent amongst *Express/Mail* readers, and by 34 per cent amongst *Sun/Star* readers, but by a mere 2 per cent amongst *Mirror* readers, which suggests the tabloids did influence their readers. *Guardian* readers swung primarily from Labour to the Alliance. *Telegraph* readers hardly swung at all. Television viewing had relatively little impact (Table 8.17).

Throughout the electorate the swing to the Conservatives was stronger amongst those who generally had relatively little interest in politics; amongst those who did not tune in to watch high-brow television or radio news; amongst those without professional qualifications; and amongst those who, despite stating a party preference in 1986, none the less denied being party 'supporters'—we can call them politically 'uncommitted'—even when they had political preferences. About half the electorate

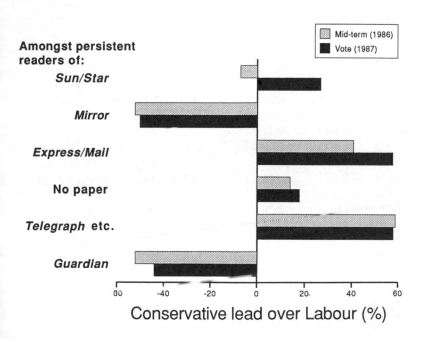

FIG. 8.4. Party Preferences in the Mid-Term and on Voting Day, by Newspaper Readership (see Table 8.17)

TABLE 8.17. *Changes in Conservative Lead over Labour 1986–1987**

	Amongst all voters	Amongst party 'supporters'	Amongst other voters
Amongst voters who persistently read			
No paper	4	0	10
Express/Mail	17	9	28
Mirror	2	2	0
Sun/Star	34	10	50
Telegraph etc.	−1	−8	10
Guardian†	8	7	11
Amongst voters who regularly watched			
Highbrow TV (or radio) news	8	1	18
No highbrow TV (or radio) news	12	7	18
ITV news only	9	16	3
BBC-TV news only	3	−3	11
Both BBC-TV and ITV news	12	6	22

Notes: This table is restricted to those who voted Conservative, Labour, or Alliance in 1987 and who declared a preference for one of those parties, or no preference at all, in 1986 (i.e. Nationalists and non-voters excluded).

Party supporters = voters who said, in 1986, that they 'supported' a party (approximately half the panel).

See also notes to Table 8.16.

* Between summer 1986 and election day, June 1987.

† Amongst *Guardian* readers, Labour support went down by 11 per cent and Conservative support by 3 per cent, while the Alliance gained 14 per cent. Since Labour lost more than the Conservatives (who had very little they could lose amongst *Guardian* readers), that produced an apparent swing to the right—but the change was not inconsistent with the *Guardian*'s politics, since the *Guardian* had traditionally backed the Liberals as its ideal first preference, though Labour as the only practical alternative to the Conservatives.

were party supporters in 1986, and half uncommitted, by this definition.

The influence of the tabloid press was particularly strong on the uncommitted. Overall, the Conservative lead increased between 1986 and June 1987 by only 5 per cent amongst party

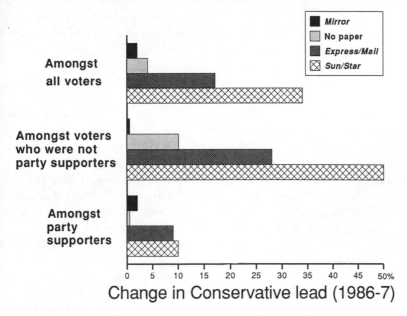

FIG. 8.5. Press Influence on Longer-Term Swings (see Table 8.17)

supporters, but by 18 per cent amongst the uncommitted. Amongst
party supporters it increased by no more than 10 per cent,
irrespective of what paper they read. But amongst uncommitted
voters, it increased by 28 per cent amongst *Express/Mail* readers
and 50 per cent amongst *Sun/Star* readers. In contrast, there
was no drift to the Conservatives amongst uncommitted *Mirror*
readers. Since *Sun/Star* readers tended to be uncommitted they
were relatively easy to influence. But that is only part of the
explanation for the magnitude of their swing to the Conservatives.
The fact that uncommitted voters who read the *Sun* or *Star* swung
so much more *than other uncommitted voters* suggests that these
papers were particularly good at influencing their readers.

Swings were highest amongst voters who watched *both* BBC
and ITV news, and amongst those who avoided watching highbrow television news programmes, but the differences between
these groups of television viewers were slight. Once we distinguished between party supporters and uncommitted voters we
found no consistent differences between voters with different
viewing habits.

Swings were highest amongst those who relied more on television than the press for help in deciding how to vote, rather lower amongst those who relied more on the press, and lowest of all amongst the 40 per cent of the electorate who found television and the press equally useful. (See Chapter 6 on who found the press and television most useful.) However, that reflected the fact that readers of highbrow papers were more likely to place their faith in the press, and they were the least likely to change their voting intentions. Amongst readers of the same paper (or paper-group as defined in Table 8.17) those who said they relied more on the press than on television were more likely to swing in the direction of their paper's partisanship: *Sun/Star* and *Express/ Mail* readers who relied more on their papers swung more strongly to the Conservatives than *Sun/Star* and *Express/Mail* readers who relied more on television; at the same time, *Mirror* readers who relied more on their paper swung towards Labour, while *Mirror* readers who relied more on television swung towards the Conservatives. While these findings are plausible enough they depend upon very small subsamples of our panel, since we have to categorize voters by their choice of paper and their reliance on the press rather than television while discarding the large numbers who relied equally on both television and the press. None the less they do seem to confirm our general findings that while television was much more informative than the press, it was much less persuasive—and intentionally so!

Though the highbrow press had the highest level of political content, it also had relatively partisan readers, and more of a mission to inform, less of a mission to persuade. On issues like unilateralism or the economy, papers like the *Guardian* and *Telegraph* did seem to influence their readers as much as the tabloids, but not on the question of voting choice. Persistent *Guardian* readers swung strongly towards a more unilateralist position, while *Telegraph* and *Times* readers swung in the opposite direction. The differences between *Mirror* and *Sun/Star* readers were in the expected directions but quite small. Similarly, on swings towards optimism about the state of the economy, the difference between *Guardian* and *Telegraph/Times* readers was greater than between *Mirror* and *Sun/Star* readers. Once again, however, differences between voters with different viewing habits were slight (Table 8.18).

TABLE 8.18. *Changes in Issue Perceptions and Attitudes 1986–1987* (%)*

	Unilateralists	Net economic optimists
Amongst voters who persistently read		
No paper	10	39
Express/Mail	6	65
Mirror	8	25
Sun/Star	−7	45
Telegraph etc.	−8	40
Guardian	17	6
Amongst voters who regularly watched		
Highbrow TV (or radio) news	6	36
No highbrow TV (or radio) news	3	42
ITV news only	10	49
BBC-TV news only	−1	34
Both BBC-TV and ITV News	4	40

Notes: See Table 8.16.

* Between summer 1986 and election day, June 1987.

CONCLUSIONS

Images of parties and party leaders are right at the margin between perceptions and attitudes. As we might expect, partisanship was a major influence upon image ratings, and it became an increasingly powerful influence as the election approached. Apart from partisanship, age also proved significant: older people had a much more favourable image of politicians of all kinds and, to a lesser extent, parties of all kinds.

Right-wing papers improved their readers' images of Thatcher and the Conservative Party, and damaged their readers' images of Kinnock and the Labour Party, though they had little or no influence upon their readers' images of the Alliance and its leaders. Press influence increased towards the end of the campaign but it remained small compared to the influence of partisanship. By the end of the campaign, Labour identifiers who read a right-wing paper were 6 per cent more favourable to Thatcher and 6 per cent less favourable to Kinnock than Labour identifiers who did not. Clearly images of parties and leaders were dominated by personal partisan prejudice and that domination increased towards the end of the campaign. None the less, there is evidence that the press had a small additional influence.

Each aspect of leader and party images varied in a different way. The press had a relatively large influence upon images of Thatcher being willing to listen, caring, and likeable. Reading right-wing papers had most effect upon improving Thatcher's image on the 'soft' virtues and damaging Kinnock's image on the 'hard' virtues—that is, on those aspects of each politician's image where they were generally considered to be at their weakest.

Political attitudes were very largely determined by partisanship, but not completely. Even with stringent controls for partisanship and ideology, multiple regression analyses show that the press, *but not television*, had a significant influence on voters' preferences. Those who read right-wing papers proved significantly more satisfied with the Conservative Party's handling of major issues, and felt significantly warmer towards Mrs Thatcher and her party. Indeed, the ideological leanings of readers' papers had more impact than their own ideology (though much less than their partisanship). The press had a particularly strong influence on the attitudes of Labour identifiers, especially towards the end of the campaign.

A year before their re-election victory the Conservatives lagged behind Labour in the opinion polls. Most of the swing back to the government occurred during the winter of 1986–7 and there was relatively little swing in the last few months before the election. We undertook a longer-term analysis, to see what part the media played in the Conservative recovery. In our panel of voters the Conservative lead over Labour increased by 34 per cent amongst *Sun/Star* readers but by a mere 2 per cent amongst *Mirror* readers, which suggests the tabloids were able to influence their readers. *Guardian* readers swung primarily from Labour to the Alliance. *Telegraph* readers hardly swung at all. Television viewing had relatively little impact.

The influence of the tabloid press was particularly strong on those voters who denied being party 'supporters', even when they had a party preference. They made up half the electorate. The Conservative lead increased by 50 per cent amongst politically uncommitted *Sun/Star* readers but not at all amongst politically uncommitted *Mirror* readers. Since *Sun/Star* readers as a whole were relatively uncommitted they were relatively easy to influence anyway but, in addition, the tabloids were particularly good at influencing their readers' voting preferences. Highbrow papers like the *Guardian* or the *Telegraph* were able to influence their readers at least as much as the tabloids on issues (like unilateralism or the economy) but not on voting choice.

9

Political Pluralism and the Media

Media analysis often arouses controversy, not just about the findings themselves but about their policy implications. Detailed summaries of this study's findings appear at the end of each chapter. But so far the conclusions have been empirical rather than moral. Right or wrong they have simply attempted to state the facts. But what are their moral implications, if any? Do our findings justify complacency or urge the need for reform. By themselves the facts are neutral but in so far as moral views about the proper role of the media are based upon presumptions about facts, our empirical findings are bound to have moral implications. By way of introduction, this chapter outlines three views about the proper role and status of the media: the *Mobilizing Ideal*, the *Libertarian Ideal*, and the *Public Service Ideal*. Other authors list a larger number of viewpoints but they seem to be relatively minor variants on these three. (McQuail, 1987, ch. 5, presents a longer list of 'ideals' or 'moral models'. There is a rough equivalence between our Libertarian and Public Service Ideals and the 'Forensic' and 'Clinical' models discussed by Wober, 1989*b*.) Then we can relate the findings of our 1987 election news study to these three ideals. This is not an attempt to deal with these ideals in a comprehensive way—no single empirical study could do that—but merely an attempt to see what bearing our factual findings may have upon moral views about the media.

THE MOBILIZING IDEAL

Views differ about the proper relationship between the mass media and society. When the invention of the printing press first allowed mass production of political pamphlets and newsletters, British governments treated them as 'seditious libels' which challenged their sovereign authority and fomented public disorder. In more recent times the behaviour of British governments has been more restrained and more sophisticated, but their instincts and suspicions remain. Conservative leader Stanley Baldwin accused the press of wanting 'power without responsibility, the prerogative of the harlot throughout the ages'. Ironically, he made the accusation in 1931 shortly before he himself exercised 'power without responsibility' as the dominant figure in Ramsay MacDonald's National Coalition government, controlling MacDonald's government without bearing the responsibility of being Prime Minister.

Authoritarians of the left, right, and centre—including right-wing dictators, old-style communists, and post-colonial governments in developing countries—have all of them espoused the Mobilizing Ideal as the proper role for the mass media. In their view, the media should be firmly subordinated to the state and its primary function should be to encourage whatever the state defines as 'good'—whether that be national consciousness and personal self-discipline, or socialist egalitarianism, or a relentless drive towards modernization and economic development. What the media should *not* do is cause friction and division within society and especially it should not encourage opposition or resistance to government decrees. It should unite rather than divide, encourage rather than discourage. Its purpose should be to mobilize support for the policies, personalities, and institutions of the regime.

Modern British governments are intellectually committed to the concepts of limited government and political pluralism, but they retain their old authoritarian instincts. Even impartiality is not welcome. During the General Strike of 1926, Winston Churchill accused the BBC of 'being impartial between the fire and the fire brigade'. Margaret Thatcher took much the same view about BBC coverage of the Falklands conflict and the troubles in Northern Ireland. Compared to overtly authoritarian regimes, British governments make relatively little use of suppression and censorship, though they do suppress some information and they do sometimes censor the media, especially on defence and security matters. More frequently they try to manipulate the media to their advantage by the selective release of carefully timed and adjusted information and by threatening, punishing, and intimidating media staff. Punishment ranges from denying interviewers access to cabinet ministers to holding down the BBC's licence fee, appointing suitable people to control both BBC and commercial broadcasting, and stimulating the public to accuse the broadcasters of bias.

It has to be emphasized that, for those who support the Mobilizing Ideal, these authoritarian features of British governments' attitudes and behaviour towards the media are not defects but virtues. They are evidence of efficient, determined, and forceful government, the alternative to which is drift, lack of authority, and chaos. Authoritarians do not apologize for the smack of firm government.

THE LIBERTARIAN IDEAL

The American Constitution is based upon the concept of liberty rather than strong, decisive government. The First Amendment declares that 'Congress shall make no law abridging the freedom of speech or of the press'. Whether Congress and the President behave in accordance with the spirit of the Constitution and the Bill of Rights is beside the point. In England, Milton argued passionately for the freedom of the press and J. S. Mill denounced the 'peculiar evil of silencing the expression of opinion'. They were defending the right of the pamphleteer to publish ideas that were unpopular in society or inconvenient for the state.

The essence of this Libertarian Ideal is that people should be free to publish what they wish and free to read or view what they wish. Some libertarians (though not perhaps Mill himself) hoped that such freedom would have consequent advantages: that it would provide a safety valve for dissent, encourage full expression of both majority and minority opinions, allow truth to drive out error, and provide some check on arbitrary misrule. But these were merely pious hopes. There is nothing about mere freedom that can guarantee anything. Permission is by definition very different from prescription (though not necessarily incompatible with it). Perhaps those who know the truth will be too lazy or too diffident or too poor to publish while whose who believe in error will be so rich, or well organized, or self-confident that they will control the presses and the television studios and dominate the 'free market in ideas'.

THE PUBLIC SERVICE IDEAL

Freedom is valuable and is valued by the public as an end in itself, but as a means to an end it has proved a failure. The fundamental strength of the Libertarian Ideal consists of nothing more than the proud assertion that freedom is an end-product that people value. Any diminution of freedom reduces the quality of life. There may be compensations for a loss of freedom but there are no substitutes for it.

On the other hand, arguments that freedom is valuable for something other than itself are seldom convincing. Usually they are a mixture of wishful thinking and libertarian special pleading. As far as British news media are concerned, freedom simply does not perform the tasks that Mill's followers hoped it would. Information is as vital to a democratic regime as propaganda is to an authoritarian one (Blumler, 1987). Yet freedom for publishers does not guarantee the adequately informed public required by democratic theory (Newton, 1988c).

In modern Britain, a mere six publishers now account for 80 per cent of all daily, Sunday, and local newspaper sales (Coxall and Robins, 1989, p. 312). Whale (1977, p. 80) has justified un-regulated commercial control of the press by arguing that 'a newspaper controlled by a commercial group writes inhibitedly about a handful of concerns at most; a paper owned by the state, the effective alternative, would be guarded in its outlook on whole areas of the national life'. His critique of the alternative is more convincing than his defence of the status quo. His argument is that newspapers may be inhibited about discussing the commercial interests of their proprietors but otherwise they exercise independent judgement. In particular there is anecdotal evidence to show that they are willing to expose the faults of other companies, including those that buy advertising space in the paper. But Whale is wrong. A newspaper controlled by a conglomerate multinational business is inhibited in discussing large areas of business. More important, it is inhibited in supporting political causes which clash with the politics of its proprietor. The largest-selling newspapers in Britain are owned by swash-buckling businessmen who do not hesitate to interfere with the editorial content of their papers and whose personal politics are so well known to all their staff that the proprietors can set the political tone of their employees' work *without* crude, direct, and explicit interference. Journalists and editors know what will please the proprietor and what will displease. But in addition, despite controlling their staff by maintaining a high personal profile on political issues, proprietors also act directly. Murdoch prides himself on being a journalist with the skill to edit his papers personally as and when he chooses. Maxwell does not have the same depth of journalistic background but none the less occasionally issues a signed 'message from the proprietor' on the front page of his papers. As a journalist himself, Hetherington (1985) emphasizes the role of editors as well as proprietors and defends their 'honest journalism' and willingness to resist both proprietorial and government pressure. But even he notes that Maxwell would telephone 'as often as six times in an evening to staff who were working on political reports'. He quotes Maxwell himself as boasting 'I sure as hell have got control and everybody knows it' (Hetherington, 1985, pp. 28–9). To suggest that press barons only influence their papers on a 'handful' of mainly commercial concerns is totally misleading. Indeed, the motivations of press barons have seldom been purely commercial (Jenkins, 1986).

The primitive concept of the Libertarian Ideal originally asserted the right of individuals and groups to voice (perhaps literally) their opinion in the market-place and to distribute their pamphlets and newsletters to those who passed by. We have to ask whether today's press or television is the modern equivalent of the speech and the pamphlet or the modern equivalent of the market-place itself. When technical or commercial factors limit the number of significant publishing organizations to a handful of major companies freedom, variety, and debate may have to be internalized *within* them. There simply are not enough competing news organizations to provide adequate variety and debate *between* them, and the technical or commercial factors that hinder the creation of rival news organizations mean that free speech cannot be guaranteed by *open entry* into a system of competing news organizations. Freedom, variety, and debate may have to be provided by open access into existing news products (existing papers, existing television networks) and by variety and debate within these products.

The Public Service Ideal is based upon the realization that the limited set of existing news sources are no longer pamphlets distributed in the market-place, they are the market-place itself; no longer speakers in a public debate, but the platform on which that debate must take place.

Within Britain, the Libertarian Ideal has traditionally been associated with the press and the Public Service Ideal with broadcasting. The reason for that is simple. There appears to be a wide variety of newspapers available to the public (even though appearances deceive), and it has always been possible in principle (if not in practice) to found a new paper. By contrast, radio and television broadcasting began and remained a monopoly or near monopoly, subject to government licensing and control, until the 1980s. With the exception of Radio Luxembourg's popular entertainment programmes, few British people ever listened to foreign broadcasts.

This distinction between the press and broadcasting is now much less clear. Increasingly powerful transmitters, satellite relays, and cable systems have begun to open up the British electorate to a wider variety of broadcast news sources, while business mergers have effectively consolidated control of the press into a very few hands (Newton, 1988a, p. 314; Negrine, 1989, ch. 4). This has made it a little more possible to contemplate a Libertarian Ideal for television, but even more necessary to consider a Public Service Ideal for the press. While new technology has reduced the costs of entry into newspaper publishing, its main effect has been to improve the profitability of established press barons. The range of newspapers read by the bulk of the British electorate has narrowed sharply over the last two decades— in terms of the political partisanship of mass-selling papers, if not in terms of the proliferation of low-circulation titles (Newton, 1988a, p. 320; Tunstall, 1983, p. 12). Indeed, with the exception of Atlanta's Cable News Network, seen by a very small audience in Britain, even the introduction of new television technology has so far only extended the reach (if not the profitability) of Britain's existing press barons.

Of course, it can be argued that readers get the paper that they want or deserve. As Whale (1977, p. 84) argues: 'It is readers who determine the character of newspapers.' Up to a point that is correct. If there were a huge demand for a quality left-wing paper then sales of the *Guardian* would increase sharply and (less certainly) an enterprising businessman might provide another left-wing alternative. But people do not buy their paper purely for its politics. They may choose a paper for its coverage of sports and scandals and then be subjected to its coverage of politics. Overall, even if they do get the paper they want, it does not follow that they get the political coverage they want.

The Public Service Ideal does not assume, against all the evidence, that a free market will necessarily produce political access, variety, and debate; it insists upon mechanisms which aim directly at these goals rather than relying upon their being achieved as the accidental by-products of mechanisms whose primary function is to achieve quite different goals such as commercial profitability or proprietorial self-indulgence. So, those who support the Public Service Ideal advocate *specific* mechanisms designed to ensure that political coverage is wide-ranging, balanced, and impartial, as well as being independent of the state. Both BBC and IBA structures were based upon this ideal. Balance is difficult to define in simple terms and requires great sensitivity by journalists if it is to be achieved. Here we are primarily concerned about balance and impartiality between political parties, but balance between social groups and institutions, or between alternative life-styles, may also be important; so too may balance between rival factions within parties—for example during contests for party leadership, such as the 1990 contest between Heseltine and Thatcher.

Outside government, few argue against the ambitions of the Public Service Ideal, but many argue that its mechanisms are oppressive and therefore support the Libertarian Ideal. Conversely, few argue against the mechanisms (or lack of them) of the Libertarian Ideal but many reject its consequences. The Royal Commission on the Press (1977) wanted to 'transplant the public service rationale of broadcasting to the press, but was opposed to the framework of public regulation that underpins it' (Curran and Seaton, 1985, p. 297). Libertarians such as Samuel Brittan (1987) argue that regulation is no different from censorship. Yet while some regulations are equivalent to censorship, others are not. The real challenge is to devise mechanisms for extending the Public Service Ideal to the British press or to British news media as a whole while minimizing the damage to the Libertarian Ideal. That clearly requires regulations that *are* different from censorship.

THE ELECTION CONTEXT: ONCE IN FOUR YEARS

'The English people think that they are free, but in this belief they are profoundly wrong. They are free only when they are electing members of parliament. Once the election has been completed, they revert to a condition of slavery: they are nothing' (Rousseau, quoted by Pulzer, 1975, p. 18). We need not agree entirely with Rousseau in order to accept his insight that election times are special. Indeed from the standpoint of a cynical manipulator we could even invert his logic. In order to enslave the English people, we might argue, it is only necessary to enslave them at election time: once in four years is enough. Governments are well aware that a cycle of economic activity can be very advantageous provided it can be synchronized with the electoral cycle, so that booms occur at election times and recessions at non-election times. Indeed one characteristic of British democracy is that the country is normally ruled by the party that lies second or third in the opinion polls (if we take averages over all months since polls began, giving each month equal weight). The British system of popular government is thus a system of *un*popular government—a consequence of this electoral cycle.

The media implications must be obvious. Media coverage of politics near to elections is more important than media coverage at non-election times. Coxall and Robins' (1989, p. 309) apology for a Conservative-dominated press, that 'it has never shied away from criticising the Conservative Party or a Conservative Government', is misleading. The question is not just *whether* it criticizes the Conservative Party but *when* it criticizes the Conservative Party. Political balance cannot be achieved by criticizing one party during the mid-term of a parliament and another at election time. Indeed that may be a more subtle form of propaganda than a constant barrage of criticism. By criticizing the Conservative Party mid-term the right-wing press can build up a certain degree of credibility with its readers which it can then use to maximum effect by suspending criticism of the Conservative Party and increasing its attacks on Labour as the election approaches. Anecdotal evidence suggests that the tabloid press stores up suitable material for use in election campaigns. Editors do think explicitly about timing and they are not motivated merely to be the first to print a 'scoop': they keep stories until the time is ripe. Old news was certainly presented as new scandal in the 1987 election campaign.

Exactly the opposite seems to happen on television. As an election approaches, the Libertarian Ideal legitimizes a switch towards more strident press partisanship, while the Public Service Ideal encourages television to be even more careful than usual to maintain balance and impartiality. The contrast between different elements of the media driven by the competing ideals of liberty and public service increases as the election approaches.

MOBILIZATION: THE FINDINGS

Despite British television's formal commitment to impartiality and balance our content analysis of national television news revealed a significant bias towards the government (Chapter 4). Though the parties *as parties* received roughly equal treatment, the government received additional coverage *as a government* for activities that were ostensibly unconnected with the election campaign. So because the government therefore got 'two bites at the cherry' there was a pro-government bias on television. This bias was particularly strong during our Pre-Campaign Wave in March when Prime Minister Thatcher visited Moscow but it continued at a reduced level throughout the final campaign. Only the utterly naïve or the determinedly blind could believe that any government activity near to election time does not have electoral implications. Martin Harrison (1989, p. 656) accepts that television 'reporting of routine, uncontroversial activities may well give incumbent governments an inbuilt advantage' but he rejects the idea of applying the concepts of impartiality and balance to the governing party's total television coverage. He draws attention to the 'French approach of dividing time into thirds—one third each to the government, the governing parties and opposition parties'. That approach, which gives two-thirds of news coverage to the incumbent government, is reasonable, even generous, if viewed in the context of the Mobilizing Ideal which accords priority to established authority. Equally, it is unreasonable, even unacceptable, in the context of other ideals for the relationship between the media and society.

Harrison and others defend the present system with another argument. They agree that the government gets extra television coverage but argue that such coverage is not necessarily favourable. In 1987 perhaps the Prime Minister's pre-election visit to Moscow and her eve-of-election trip to the Venice summit of Western leaders were favourable to her re-election, but 'Harold Wilson always asserted that a bad set of trade figures a few days before polling cost him an election, while the effect of being centre-stage during the Iran hostages affair may have been devastating to Jimmy Carter's fortunes'. That may be true, but in 1987 hostile interviews with Neil Kinnock trying to explain his party's defence policy counted as part of the Labour Party's coverage. Coverage of *all* kinds can be both favourable and unfavourable—no matter whether politicians are in government or in opposition—and politicians themselves must bear the prime responsibility for ensuring that when they do get access to the media they present their own case well. There is no difference between government coverage and party coverage in this respect except that government has more initiative in determining the news, which means that it has more opportunity than the opposition to ensure that its coverage is favourable. So long as balance is defined in terms of the quantity of party coverage— and not whether it is favourable or unfavourable—then the only justification for awarding the government extra coverage is that the government represents order, stability, and legitimate authority, which the media has a duty to support. Those who do not approve the Mobilizing Ideal for the media should not approve extra media time for the government, especially near to election time.

Throughout the 1980s leading supporters of the Conservative government, notably Norman Tebbit and his Media Monitoring Unit, alleged left-wing bias on the BBC (Negrine, 1989, p. 123; BBC, 1986). It is difficult to see that as anything other than an attempt to intimidate the BBC. Our content analysis of national television news in Chapter 4 suggests that television news was biased both towards the government of the day (through extra coverage of the government) and towards right-wing political viewpoints (through its emphasis on crime, defence, and security). Our comparison of BBC-TV with ITV in Chapter 5 showed that there was little difference between them. Our opinion survey in Chapter 6 showed that most voters felt television news on both networks was unbiased; but amongst the minority who felt it was biased a majority thought it was biased towards the Conservatives and against both Labour and the Alliance. At the same time a large majority of voters thought that the press was biased, and that it was biased towards the Conservatives, against Labour, and against the Alliance.

Both our content analysis and our survey of public opinion suggest that allegations of anti-Conservative bias on the BBC were wildly off-target. If Tebbit wished to attack bias as such he should have directed his criticism at the press rather than television. The media certainly were biased—but *towards* the Conservative government, *not against* it; and bias was very much more evident in the press than on television. But, of course, his attack was very much on-target if he simply wished to attack those elements of the media that were least favourable to his own party and government. Though television was pro-government and pro-Conservative it was much less so than other elements of the mass media. Judged against the Mobilizing Ideal, therefore, both BBC-TV and ITV were guilty of failing to show enough enthusiasm for the government of the day.

Would it have been different under a Labour government? Under a Labour government we might expect television to be somewhat more favourable to the Labour Party. Labour would then benefit from the extra coverage given to the incumbent government. But the bias towards defence and security (which have historically been natural right-wing issues) might well persist and offset Labour's advantage as the incumbent government, unless the 1989 Year of Revolutions in Eastern Europe ushers in a new era of world peace and tranquillity. The 1990 Gulf Crisis suggests that world conflict will unfortunately continue, even though its location may shift. So under a Labour government, television would probably not be quite so pro-Labour as it was pro-Conservative under a Conservative government. A Labour government would feel the same need to mobilize support as a Conservative government and Labour politicians in office would probably feel even more disappointed with television than Conservative politicians. But the enormous contrast between *relatively* unbiased news on television and extreme pro-Conservative bias in the press would encourage Labour politicians to moderate their criticism of television and concentrate their attack on the press.

LIBERTY AND PUBLIC SERVICE: THE FINDINGS

It is ironic, but perhaps not surprising that the more virulent allegations of media bias have been levelled at the most balanced and impartial element of the media. Conservative politicians attack the BBC for its alleged left-wing bias (Newton, 1988*a*, p. 326); academic sociologists attack it for its alleged anti-trade union and pro-right-wing bias (Glasgow University Media Group, 1976, 1980, 1982; Beharrell and Philo, 1977). Our own content analysis also suggests that British television news has not, in fact, achieved its goal of perfect impartiality in absolute terms. But in relative terms there can be no doubt that British broadcasting comes close to the Public Service Ideal while the British press comes nowhere near it. Indeed most of the British press does not seek to do so. Unlike the American press, where papers serve geographically defined communities, the English press operates on a national scale and serves social groups or campaigning proprietors rather than complete communities. (The Scottish press is more like the American in this respect.) That encourages the English press to take a divisive, partisan line.

The British electorate have no illusions about press balance. Only a small minority of voters in our panel thought that television was biased and they were not agreed upon the direction of that bias. But a large majority of newspaper readers felt that their own papers were biased. A majority of readers of every one of the major-selling papers thought their own paper was biased—not just readers of the tabloids but readers of quality papers such as the *Telegraph* and the *Guardian*.

We found evidence that the electors exercised a coherent choice amongst the media sources on offer; and that they enjoyed exercising that choice. There was real choice available in terms of depth and detail, ranging from entertaining but uninformative tabloids to highbrow news sources like the quality papers, Radio 4 news, or television programmes like *Newsnight* and *Channel 4 News*. Highbrow sources were clearly much more attractive to people who were particularly interested in politics. Younger voters tended towards the tabloid press and Radios 1 and 2. Highbrow papers and highbrow radio were particularly sought after by the highly educated. Highbrow television, however, reached the politically interested almost irrespective of their education level. These variations in media use suggest that radio and the press provide a choice of detail which matches the demands of different sectors of the public—in keeping with the Libertarian Ideal. At the same time the audience pattern for highbrow television news seems more in keeping with the Public Service Ideal: reaching out to the interested public irrespective of social background.

There was much less choice in terms of the media's political partisanship. Only the *Guardian* amongst the qualities and the *Mirror* (with its Scottish stable-mate, the *Record*) amongst the tabloids could be considered even moderately left-wing in 1987. Even the *Guardian* had advocated a Conservative victory, albeit with a 'small majority', in 1983 (Roberts, 1989, p. 37). Left-wingers were clearly more attracted to left-wing papers, particularly during the election campaign, but the poverty of partisan choice meant that many left-wing voters read right-wing papers. The range of available papers, judged by their partisanship, was inadequate for either the Libertarian or Public Service Ideals, though left-wing perspectives were articulated by a small minority of the press.

Choice of television viewing was even more limited partly by the similarity between BBC-TV and ITV, but also by the electorate's tendency to watch *both* BBC-TV and ITV. Judged by the Public Service Ideal, television did well, though it fell short of perfection. Variety existed within television programmes. Though the news was at least relatively balanced and impartial, the balance was achieved by giving time and attention to a variety of alternative viewpoints, not by suppressing diversity. None the less, viewers seemed to resent their lack of choice and lack of control over what they saw. The variety of television news (and current affairs) programmes allowed them to choose the degree of depth and detail they wanted, but not the political viewpoints expressed. In Britain, unlike some European countries, there is no choice between a right-wing and a left-wing television news channel. So while television scored well in terms of public service, it scored less well in terms of freedom of choice.

While voters generally thought that television was unbiased and that the press was biased we found that allegations of bias were not synonymous with disapproval. Partisan viewers tended to see television as being *less* favourable to their own party than it appeared to be in the eyes of other viewers. In other words, general perceptions of bias (or the lack of it) were overlaid by a tendency for viewers to *react against* television news, alleging that it was biased towards their opponents. At the same time, partisan readers tended to claim that their newspaper was *more* favourable to their own party than it appeared to be in the eyes of other readers. So generally clear perceptions of strong press bias were overlaid by a tendency for readers to claim that their paper was relatively sympathetic to their own political viewpoint. Right-wing readers of a right-wing paper were *more* likely than left-wing readers of that same paper to claim that their paper was biased towards the right—though a majority of both left- and right-wing readers typically agreed that their papers were biased and agreed on the direction of that bias. Instead of reacting against the bias in their chosen paper, readers tended (at the margin) to defend their paper (if it was biased against their party) or even to glory in its bias (if it was biased in favour of their party).

The difference between public responses to perceptions of bias in the press and on television was reflected in the complex relationship between voters' allegations of bias and their ratings of the 'usefulness' of the press and television news. Viewers who alleged bias on television tended to give television news *lower* marks for 'usefulness' than viewers who perceived no bias on television; but readers who alleged bias in their papers tended to give their papers *higher* marks for 'usefulness' than readers who perceived no bias in their paper (Chapter 6).

Overall, although readers were well aware that their papers were relatively biased compared to television and although they rated television as much more useful for providing information about issues, they did *not* rate television much more useful in helping them decide how to vote. Their perceptions of press bias did not prompt readers to reject press guidance.

It is perhaps significant that there appeared to be more choice of newspaper than of television news. To the general public, newspapers were visibly different in tone, style, and partisan bias, even though media analysts know that this apparent variety is controlled and constrained by a handful of publishers. By contrast, television news is produced by only two networks (each broadcasting on two channels) which are constrained by law to offer remarkably similar products, however balanced, internally varied, and impartial those products might be. National television news originates—and was seen to originate—from either the newsroom at the BBC's London Television Centre or the newsroom of ITN, which supplies both ITV and Channel 4 news. Voters who read a stridently left- or right-wing paper are at least exercising some choice, even if their own partisanship is different from that of their paper. But any bias they detect on television is inflicted upon them by what seems like a television news cartel. Impartiality can be irritating to viewers as well as to governments— though much less so to viewers. The Libertarian Ideal is seductive.

Previous studies have repeatedly drawn attention to the fact that voters, particularly those who read lowbrow tabloids, tend to believe the news on television but remain sceptical about what they read in the press (see, for example, Negrine, 1989, p. 3). Our study confirms that finding but questions its relevance and its implications. Despite their scepticism, readers said they found the press useful, particularly for guiding their voting decision if not for providing information. Academics regard bias as a sin, but others may regard it as a virtue. In the real world of politics the distinction between 'bias' and 'commitment' is not always clear.

Our analyses of voters' information levels and their changing political preferences confirm and even strengthen that finding. Once personal circumstances were taken into account, people's information levels were influenced primarily by how much television news they watched while their swings of political preferences were influenced primarily by which newspaper they read (Chapters 7 and 8).

Frequent television viewers were significantly more aware of opinion poll findings, more aware of party leaders' activities, more aware of second-rank politicians' activities, and more aware of the parties' campaign themes. Watching television news also made viewers feel more warmth towards parties and their leaders generally (that is, towards any and all parties) and more inclined to vote (for any and all parties). At the same time, readers of right-wing papers were significantly more inclined to be optimistic about the economy, had a significantly better image of the Conservative Party and its leader, gave the Conservative Party better ratings for handling issues, felt more warmth towards the Conservative Party, and swung more strongly towards voting Conservative.

So despite the speculations of sociologists, television did not trivialize the news nor generate alienation and apathy. Quite the contrary. It did a particularly good job of informing people about the issues—especially if they were tabloid press readers, who could get relatively little information from the press; and it made electors feel more warmth and commitment to the party system and party leaders generally. What it did not do was encourage people to discriminate between rival politicians and parties. That remained much more a function of the press.

Also contrary to the speculations of media sociologists, television not only failed to determine what the electorate thought, it also failed to determine what they thought *about*, though it did communicate to the electorate what the parties were fighting about. Television failed to 'set the public agenda' in 1987, though it succeeded in 'communicating the party agenda'. Television's enormous shift of emphasis on to defence issues in the third week of the campaign correlated with a huge rise in the number of voters who saw defence as the Conservative Party's main campaign theme, but with only a modest rise in the number of who wanted a defence debate. The switch of news focus clearly had *some* influence on the public's agenda but a remarkably small one: in terms of television influencing the public's agenda the cause seemed much greater than the effect.

ONCE IN FOUR YEARS: THE FINDINGS

A major theme that ran through our findings was the enormous difference between election and non-election times. In the mid-term between elections interest in politics was much higher amongst highly educated voters and amongst regular readers of the quality press the *Guardian*, the *Telegraph*, *The Times*, and similar papers. But that was no longer true at election time: as the election approached the highly educated became less interested and the less well educated became more interested (Chapter 2). Those who remained uninterested in politics reacted by avoiding the news during the campaign. On any day towards the end of the campaign, those who had been very interested in politics just before the campaign opened were one and a half times as likely to read a paper, and twice as likely to watch both BBC-TV and ITV news, as those with no interest in politics (Chapter 3).

As the election approached, voters' awareness of opinion polls became less dependent upon their interest in politics and on whether they read the highbrow press rather than the tabloids. Instead it became more dependent upon how frequently they watched television news. The same was true for the electorate's awareness of party leaders. Even their awareness of second-rank leaders came to depend more upon television viewing though, in this case, no less upon their interest in politics and their access to the quality press. Particularly at election time, television reached out and informed sections of the electorate which were usually much less well informed about politics. Television reached those parts of the electorate that other high-quality news sources could not reach.

Also as the campaign drew to a close, partisan voters alleged more *unfavourable* bias on television news and more *favourable* bias in their daily papers. No doubt both tendencies arose in part because the voters themselves became more strongly partisan at that time; but it also seems likely that television became more strictly impartial (thereby offending both Labour and Conservative partisans more) while the press became more stridently partisan (Chapter 6).

As the election approached readers of right-wing tabloids, particularly those who had had weak or non-existent party preferences in the mid-term, swung heavily towards the Conservatives while other readers did not. Most of that swing occurred between our Mid-Term Wave of interviews in the early summer of 1986 and our Pre-Campaign Wave in March 1987. During the final campaign itself swings in voting preferences were relatively small, but the change between the mid-term and election day was large.

Overall television fulfilled its public service role of informing the electorate, and did so particularly well as the election drew closer; while the press fulfilled its self-assigned role as pamphleteers within a libertarian system, and did so with increasing effect as the election drew closer.

PRESCRIPTIONS

Supporters of the Libertarian Ideal must be pleased by the degree of public satisfaction with the press despite public perceptions of press bias. Indeed they must be pleased by the traces of evidence that suggest that bias in a freely chosen medium such as a newspaper is actually popular with the electorate rather than resented. Similarly they must be pleased by the traces of evidence that suggest partisan voters find the relative impartiality of television news somewhat irritating. They will advocate the deregulation of broadcasting and the proliferation of channels.

If they hoped that freedom would automatically bring intellectual variety and competition they must be disappointed with the press and pessimistic about the effects of deregulation on broadcasting, however. Perhaps, for them, the introduction of a variety of deliberately partisan television channels might be a more attractive if less than perfect solution. It would give the viewer freedom of choice, even if that freedom was not extended to the broadcasters. It might require public subsidies to political parties to finance their own newspapers and television stations. Alternatively, rival parties could be given control of different public television stations: so BBC 1 and Channel 4 might become 'conservative-right wing' channels while BBC 2 and ITV become 'socialist-left wing' channels, which could then compete for an audience. The situation in some European countries approximates that model. In Britain the idea of openly partisan broadcasting was pioneered by the Scottish Nationalists' clandestine and illegal Radio Free Scotland in the 1960s and more recently by Southern Sound, who used a discarded former commercial radio band to set up their entirely open and legal Conference Radio FM to cover the 1990 Conservative Party Conference from an unashamedly pro-Conservative viewpoint.

Supporters of the Public Service Ideal will be disappointed by our finding that television news is biased towards the incumbent government, and alarmed by our evidence that the tabloid press has such a powerful influence over its readers at election time. For them, the solution to the problem of pro-government bias is simple: the broadcasters should treat government and governing party as one and the same, and give it the same coverage as the main opposition party. The problem of an influential tabloid press heavily biased towards one particular party is more difficult. One solution would be to extend regulation to the press to ensure the same kind of impartiality as on television. The Royal Commission rejected that solution as too oppressive, smacking of government censorship.

However, it would be possible to require all newspapers with a mass circulation (say, for example, half a million copies) to carry, without payment, the equivalent of television's Party Election Broadcasts—that is, pages of free advertising in the same party ratio as PEBs on television. Sceptics may doubt whether anyone would read it but our survey shows that viewers take PEBs seriously and rate them only slightly less useful than news broadcasts for helping decide how to vote (though much less useful than news broadcasts for providing information). That would not in any way restrict the paper's right to print whatever it wished in the rest of the paper. Free and regulated newspaper advertising would also help to reduce the dependence of party politics on large trade union, business, or private donations; and the press could take some satisfaction, if no profit, from their public service contribution to an informed democracy.

Alternatively, the public service rules for television impartiality could be changed to require balance throughout the mass media as a whole. The press would be left to adopt whatever political positions it wished, but television would be required to adjust its coverage to ensure that television plus the press, taken together, were politically balanced. So when the press was biased towards the political right, television coverage would redress the balance by leaning to the left. Conversely, if the press swung heavily to the left, television would have to reorient its coverage and redress the balance by leaning to the right. (For an extended discussion of alternative approaches to media reform see Curran, 1986.)

These are radical suggestions which may seem impractical; but the status quo may be indefensible. Satellite television stations under the control of press barons and modelled on the tabloid press may make inaction even more indefensible. Those who support the Public Service Ideal could accept the combination of a polyarchic press putting forward a multitude of rival viewpoints and an impartial, balanced broadcasting monopoly. That would produce both balance and variety in the media taken as a whole. But by the same logic they cannot accept the combination of a press controlled by a handful of publishers, overwhelmingly biased in one direction, and impartial, balanced broadcasting. Still less can they accept impartial public broadcasting combined with a biased press and biased satellite television. If balance is important it cannot be limited to public television.

APPENDIX

Explanation of the Terms 'Party Identification', 'Partisan' 'Party Supporter', and 'Party Preference'

The concept of 'party identification' was first used in voting studies by Lazarsfeld *et al.* (1944), Berelson *et al.* (1954), and later popularized by Campbell *et al.* (1954, 1960). It denotes the voter's psychological sense of belonging, commitment, or loyalty towards a party. It is a measure of the voter's general, normal, usual, or habitual party choice and can be contrasted with their specific choice on any one occasion. So, for example, we can discuss not only Labour identifiers' political attitudes, but also their votes or voting preferences since, on any one occasion, some people who generally think of themselves as Labour may decide to vote against 'their' party's candidate. Such a tendency was particularly marked in 1983 when many voters declared a Labour identification but voted Alliance, Conservative, or not at all. We use the term 'partisan' as an abbreviation for 'party identifier'.

Different surveys use different questions to measure what is essentially the same concept. Lazarsfeld *et al.*'s original question read: 'Regardless of how you may vote in the coming election how have you *usually* thought of yourself—as a Republican, Democrat, Socialist, or what?' Campbell *et al.*'s version, which (suitably modified) became very widely used in Britain as well as the USA, read: '*Generally* speaking, do you usually consider yourself a Republican, a Democrat, an Independent, or what?' Both Lazarsfeld *et al.* and Campbell *et al.* followed their questions about the direction of party identification with a question about the strength of party identification, so that they could distinguish 'strong partisans' from 'weak parisans'. For a full discussion of these classic American election studies see Miller (1983).

Recently, the British Social Attitudes Survey (Jowell *et al.*, 1987) has used a different question which reads: '*Generally* speaking, do you think of yourself as a *supporter* of any one political party? Which?' This is quite strong language. Those who describe themselves as 'supporters' are roughly equivalent to the 'strong partisans' of the American studies, rather than to all the party identifiers (including both 'strong' and 'weak' partisans). Those who denied being party supporters were then asked: 'Do you think of yourself as *a little closer* to one political party than to the others? Which?' We use the term 'party leaners' to denote those who were not 'supporters' but did feel 'a little closer' to one party than to others. 'Leaners' plus 'supporters', taken together, are roughly equivalent to the 'party identifiers' (weak and strong) of the classic American studies. Finally, those who denied feeling even 'a little closer' to a party were asked their current voting preference. In our Mid-Term Wave, which was part of the 1986 British Social Attitudes Survey (BSAS), approximately half the sample described themselves as 'party supporters', another quarter were 'party leaners', and most, but not all, of the rest had at least a current preference.

We continued to use the BSAS questions about 'supporters' and 'leaners' in the later waves of our campaign study, but we asked everyone (including supporters and leaners) about their current voting preferences, using a different question format. The text of this book uses terms as follows.

Party supporters: only those who described themselves as a 'supporter' of a party.

Party identifiers (or *partisans*): 'supporters' plus 'leaners'.

Party preferences: all those with a party preference; in the Mid-Term Wave (BSAS) this is based on a combination of 'supporter', 'leaner', and 'preference' questions; in other waves this is based upon a separate question about voting intentions.

We asked all party 'supporters' to say 'how strongly' they supported their chosen party: 'very', 'fairly', or 'not very' strongly. That provides a six-point scale for 'strength of partisanship' ('partisanship' for short) ranging as follows:

1. Very strong party supporters (strongest)
2. Fairly strong party supporters
3. Not very strong party supporters
4. Party leaners ('a little closer')
5. Those with only voting preferences
6. Those without any preferences (weakest)

This six-point scale can be simplified by combining adjacent categories to produce, for example, a three-point scale. The text makes clear how this has been done in particular analyses. Where the term 'partisanship' is used in correlation and regression tables in this book it is always an abbreviation for 'strength of partisanship', never for 'direction of partisanship'.

Pre-Wave Questionnaire (March–April 1987)

QC100: Generally speaking, do you think of yourself as a *supporter* of any one political party?

Yes	1
No	2
DK/Depends	9

IF YES: Which? ———— SUPPORTS:

Conservative	1
Labour	2
Liberal	3
Social Democrats	4
Alliance	4
Nationalist	6
Other (SPECIFY) ————	7
Won't say which	8

If YES: And how *strongly* do you support that party?

very strongly?	1
fairly strongly?	2
not very strongly?	3
DK/NA	9

IF NO/DK: Do you think of yourself as a *little closer* to one political party than to the others?

LITTLE CLOSER TO: Conservative	1
Labour	2
Liberal	3
Social Democrats	4
Alliance	5
Nationalist	6
Other (SPECIFY) ————	7
No/None	8
DK/NA	9

REFERENCES

American Enterprise (1990), 'The American Enterprise Public Opinion Report', July/August, 95.

AXFORD, B., and MADGWICK, P. (1986), *Television News Monitoring Project April–June 1986: Second Report* (Oxford: Oxford Polytechnic).

—— —— (1989), 'Indecent exposure? Three party politics in television news during the 1987 general election', in Crewe and Harrop (1989).

BARNES, S., and KAASE, M. (eds.) (1979), *Political Action: Mass Participation in Five Western Democracies* (Beverly Hills, Calif.: Sage).

BBC (1986), *The Conservative Central Office Media Monitoring* (London: BBC, Nov.).

—— (1987), *Public Reactions to BBC and ITV Coverage of the 1987 General Election* (London: BBC, Nov.).

—— (1988), *BBC Television Facts and Figures 1988* (London: BBC).

BEHARRELL, P., and PHILO, G. (eds.) (1977), *Trade Unions and the Media* (London: Macmillan).

BERELSON, B. (1959), 'The state of communication research', *Public Opinion Quarterly*, 23: 1–6.

—— LAZARSFELD, P. F., and McPHEE, W. N. (1954), *Voting: A Study of Opinion Formation in a Presidential Campaign* (Chicago: Chicago University Press).

BLUMLER, J. G. (1987), 'Election communication and the democratic political system', in Paletz, 1987.

—— and GUREVITCH, M. (1986), *The Election-Agenda-Setting Roles of Television Journalists: Comparative Observation at the BBC and NBC* (Chicago: Conference of International Communication Association, May 1986).

—— —— and IVES, J. (1978), *The Challenge of Election Broadcasting* (Leeds: Leeds University Press).

—— —— and NOSSITER, T. J. (1986), 'Setting the television news agenda: campaign observation at the BBC', in Crewe and Harrop, 1986.

—— —— —— (1989), 'The earnest versus the determined: election newsmaking at the BBC, 1987', in Crewe and Harrop, 1989.

—— and KATZ, E. (eds.) (1974), *The Uses of Mass Communication: Current Perspectives of Gratifications Research* (Beverly Hills, Calif.: Sage).

—— and McQUAIL, D. (1968), *Television in Politics: Its Uses and Influence* (London: Faber).

BRITTAN, S. (1987), 'The fight for freedom in broadcasting', *Political Quarterly*, 58: 3–23.

BUDGE, I., and FARLIE, D. J.(1983), *Explaining and Predicting Elections* (London: Allen and Unwin).

BUTLER, D. (1989), *British General Elections since 1945* (Oxford: Blackwell).

—— and KAVANAGH, D. (1988), *The British General Election of 1987* (London: Macmillan).

—— and STOKES, D. (1969), *Political Change in Britain* (London: Macmillan; 2nd edn. 1975).

CAMPBELL, A., GURIN, G., and MILLER, W. E. (1954), *The Voter Decides* (Evanston, Ill. Row Paterson).

—— CONVERSE, P. E., MILLER, W. E., and STOKES, D. E. (1960), *The American Voter* (New York: Wiley).

CHAFFEE, S., and BERGER, C. (eds.) (1987), *The Handbook of Communication Science* (London: Sage).

—— and SCHLEUDER, J. (1986), 'Measurement and effects of attention to media news', *Human Communication Research*, 13: 76–107.

CREWE, I., and HARROP, M.(eds.) (1986), *Political Communications: The General Election Campaign of 1983* (Cambridge: Cambridge University Press).

—— —— (eds.) (1989), *Political Communications: The General Election Campaign of 1987* (Cambridge: Cambridge University Press).

COXALL, B., and ROBINS, L. (1989), *Contemporary British Politics* (London: Macmillan), ch. 14, 'The Mass Media'.

CURRAN, J. (1986), 'The different approaches to media reform', in Curran *et al.*, 1986.

—— ECCLESTONE, J., OAKLEY, G., and RICHARDSON, A. (eds.) (1986), *Bending Reality* (London: Pluto Press).

—— and Seaton, J. (1985), *Power without Responsibility: The Press and Broadcasting in Britain* (London: Fontana).

DRUCKER, H., DUNLEAVY, P., GAMBLE, A., and PEELE, G. (eds.) (1988), *Developments in British Politics*, ii (London: Macmillan).

DYE, T. R., and ZEIGLER, L. H.(1983), *American Politics in the Media Age* (Belmont, Calif. Wadsworth).

Economist, The (1990), 'The economy: a thousand cuts', 16–22 June, 34–9.

Glasgow University Media Group (1976), *Bad News* (London: Routledge).

—— (1980), *More Bad News* (London: Routledge).

—— (1982) *Really Bad News* (London: Writers and Readers).

GUNTER, B., SVENNEVIG, M., and WOBER, M. (1984), 'Viewers' experience of television coverage of the 1983 general election', *Parliamentary Affairs*, 37: 279.

—— —— —— (1986) *Television Coverage of the 1983 General Election: Audiences, Appreciation and Public Opinion* (Aldershot: Gower).

HARRISON, M. (1988), 'Broadcasting', in Butler and Kavanagh, 1988.

—— (1989), 'Television election news analysis: use and abuse—a reply', *Political Studies*, 37: 652–8.

HARROP, M. (1986), 'The press and post-war elections', in Crewe and Harrop, 1986.
—— (1987), 'Voters', in Seaton and Pimlott, 1987*b*.
—— (1988), 'The Press', in Butler and Kavanagh, 1988.
HETHERINGTON, A. (1985), *News, Newspapers and Television* (London: Macmillan).
—— (1989*a*), 'Two sides of the border: reporting the campaign in Scotland', in Crewe and Harrop, 1989.
—— (1989*b*), *News in the Regions: Plymouth Sound to Moray Firth* (London: Macmillan).
HOLLINGSWORTH, M. (1986), *The Press and Political Dissent: A Question of Censorship* (London: Pluto).
IBA (1987), *Attitudes to Broadcasting in 1986* (London: Independent Broadcasting Authority Research Department).
IYENGAR, S., and KINDER, D. R.(1987), *News That Matters: Television and American Opinion* (Chicago: University of Chicago Press).
JENKINS, S.(1986), *The Market for Glory: Fleet Street Ownership in the Twentieth Century* (London: Faber).
JOWELL, R., WITHERSPOON, S., and BROOK, L. (eds.) (1987), *British Social Attitudes* (Aldershot: Gower).
JOWETT, G. S., and O'DONNELL, V. (1986), *Propaganda and Persuasion* (London: Sage).
KATZ, E., and LAZARSFELD, P. F. (1955), *Personal Influence* (Glencoe, Ill.: Free Press).
KELLNER, P., and WORCESTER, R. (1982), 'Electoral perceptions of media stance', in Worcester and Harrop, 1982.
KLAPPER, J. T.(1960), *The Effects of Mass Communication* (Glencoe, Ill.: Free Press).
KLINE, F. G., and TICHENER, P. J. (eds.) (1972), *Current Perspectives in Mass Communication Research* (London: Sage).
KRAUS, S. (ed.) (1979), *The Great Debates: Carter vs. Ford 1976* (Bloomington, Ind.: Indiana University Press).
LASSWELL, H D. (1927), *Propaganda Technique in the World War* (New York: Knopf).
LAZARSFELD, P. F., BERELSON, B., and GAUDET, H. (1944), *The People's Choice: How the Voter Makes up his Mind in a Presidential Campaign* (New York: Duell, Sloan, and Pearce; 2nd edn., New York: Columbia University Press, 1948).
LIPPMANN, W. (1922), *Public Opinion* (New York: Macmillan).
MACARTHUR, B. (1989), 'The national press', in Crewe and Harrop, 1989.
McCOMBS, M. E., and SHAW, D. L. (1972), 'The agenda-setting function of the press', *Public Opinion Quarterly*, 36: 176–87.
McGREGOR, R., SVENNEVIG, M., and LEDGER, C. (1989), 'Television and the 1987 general election campaign', in Crewe and Harrop, 1989.

McLeod, J. M. (1988), 'The mass media and citizenship' (Glasgow: Glasgow University Stevenson Lecture, May 1988).

—— and Becker, L. B. (1974), 'Testing the validity of gratification measures through political effects analysis', in Blumler and Katz, 1974.

—— —— and Byrnes, J. (1974), 'Another look at the agenda setting function of the press', *Communication Research*, 1: 131–66.

—— and Blumler, J. G. (1987), 'The macrosocial level of communication science', in Chaffee and Berger, 1987.

—— Durall, J. A., Ziemke, D. A., and Bybee, C. R. (1979), 'Reactions of younger and older voters: Expanding the context of effects', in Kraus, 1979.

—— Pan, Z., and Sun, S. (1990), 'Cognitive and Affective Bases of Voting' (Dublin: Paper to Conference of International Communication Association, May 1990).

McQuail, D. (1987), *Mass Communication Theory* (London: Sage).

Miller, W. L. (1983), *The Survey Method in the Social and Political Sciences* (London: Pinter).

—— Clarke, H. D., Harrop, M., LeDuc, L., and Whiteley, P. F. (1990), *How Voters Change: The 1987 British Election Campaign in Perspective* (Oxford: Clarendon Prress).

Negrine, R. (1989), *Politics and the Mass Media in Britain* (London: Routledge).

Newton, K. (1988a), 'Mass Media', in Drucker *et al.*, 1988.

—— (1988b), 'Politics and the media', *Political Studies*, 36: 696–703.

—— (1988c), *Liberal Neutrality and the News Media* (Essex: University of Essex Papers in Politics and Government, No. 53).

—— (1990), 'Making news: the mass media in Britain', *Social Studies Review*, 6: 12–15.

O'Shaughnessy, N. J. (1990), *The Phenomenon of Political Marketing* (London: Macmillan).

Paletz, D. L. (ed.) (1987), *Political Communication Research: Approaches, Studies, Assessments* (Norwood, NJ: Ablex).

Patterson, T. E. (1980), *The Mass Media Election* (New York: Praeger).

Piepe, A., Charlton, P., and Morey, J. (1988), *Political Mainstreaming in England: Hegemony or Pluralism?* (Portsmouth: Portsmouth Polytechnic Media Research Group).

Pilsworth, M. (1986), 'Set TV free and let the people see', in Crewe and Harrop, 1986.

Pulzer, P. G. J. (1975), *Political Representation and Elections in Britain* (London: Allen and Unwin).

Roberts, D. (ed.) (1989), *Discovering Politics* (Ormskirk: Causeway Press).

ROBINSON, J. P. (1972), 'Mass communication and information diffusion', in Kline and Tichener, 1972.

Royal Commission on the Press 1974–77 (1977), *Cmnd. 6810* (London: HMSO).

SEATON, J., and PIMLOTT, B. (1987*a*), 'The struggle for balance', in Seaton and Pimlott, 1987*b*).

—— —— (eds.) (1987*b*), *The Media in British Politics* (Aldershot: Avebury).

SEYMOUR-URE, C. K. (1974), *The Political Impact of Mass Media* (London: Constable).

SHAW, D. L., and McCOMBS, M. (1977), *The Emergence of American Political Issues: The Agenda-Setting Function of the Press* (St Paul, Minn.: West).

TRENAMAN, J. S. M., and McQUAIL, D. (1961), *Television and the Political Image* (London: Methuen).

TUNSTALL, J. (1983), *The Media in Britain* (London: Constable).

TYLER, R. (1987), *Campaign: The Selling of the Prime Minister* (London: Grafton).

VERBA, S., NIE, N. H., and KIM, J. (1978), *Participation and Political Equality: A Seven Nation Comparison* (New York: Cambridge University Press).

WEAVER, D., WILHOIT, C., and SEMETKO, H. (1986), *The Role of the Press in the Formation of Campaign Agendas in Britain and the United States* (Chicago: Conference of International Communication Association, May 1986).

WHALE, J. (1977), *The Politics of the Media* (London: Fontana).

WHITE, S. (1990), *Gorbachev in Power* (Cambridge: Cambridge University Press).

WOBER, M. (1989*a*), 'Party political and election broadcasts 1985–87: their perceived attributes and impact upon viewers', in Crewe and Harrop, 1989.

—— (1989*b*), *The Use and Abuse of Television* (Hove: Erlbaum Associates).

WORCESTER, R., and HARROP, M. (eds.) (1982), *Political Communications: The General Election Campaign of 1979* (London: Allen and Unwin).

INDEX